6 an
6.—
B.F.2o.1

Sailing
Solo
to
America

Alain Colas, winner of the Observer Transatlantic Race 1972

Sailing
Solo
to
America

by Frank Page

Quadrangle Books, Inc.
New York Times Company

Library of Congress Card Number: 70-190133

ISBN 0 8129 0298 X

Printed in Great Britain

Acknowledgements

The author wishes to thank the following: Sir Francis Chichester, *Alone Across the Atlantic*, George Allen & Unwin and Doubleday; H W Tilman, *'Mischief' in Patagonia*, Cambridge University Press; Chay Blyth, *The Impossible Voyage*, Hodder & Stoughton and G P Putnams & Sons; Dr David Lewis, *Daughters of the Wind*, Victor Gollancz; Robin Knox-Johnston, *A World of My Own*, Cassell and William Morrow; Robert Manry, *Tinkerbelle*, William Collins Sons and Brandt & Brandt; Charles A Borden, *Sea Quest*, Robert Hale; Tomalin and Hall, *The Strange Voyage of Donald Crowhurst*, Hodder & Stoughton and Stein & Day; Vito Dumas, *Alone Through the Roaring Forties*, Adlard Coles Ltd; J R L Anderson, *The Ulysses Factor*, Hodder & Stoughton and Harcourt Brace Jovanovich; Humphrey Barton, *Atlantic Adventures*, Adlard Coles Ltd; Geoffrey Williams, *Sir Thomas Lipton Wins*, Peter Davies and Lippincott; Joshua Slocum, *Sailing Alone Around the World*, Mariners Library, Adlard Coles Ltd; S Pakenham, *Separate Horizons*, Nautical Publishing; Eric Tabarly, *Lonely Victory*, Souvenir Press and Clarkson & Potter; Alain Gerbault, *The Fight of the Firecrest, In Quest of the Sun*, Mariners Library, Adlard Coles Ltd.

Contents

Illustrations

For Sam

Foreword

The fourth Observer Singlehanded Transatlantic Race, sailed in the summer of 1972, may one day prove to have been the most important race in the whole series. For the first time we seemed to have created an important international sailing event with more than enough entries, with an extraordinary diversity in size and type of boat, and yet without that lunatic element of unseaworthy boats and embarrassing skippers that had made the 1968 race a bonanza for the world's press and a big headache for the Race Committee of the Royal Western Yacht Club.

For the first time that committee may now have to concern itself with limiting the number of starters, and perhaps with discouraging the entry of excessively large boats whose success may be against the best interests of the race itself. As the competitive pressures increase it is inevitable that new rules of this sort will have to be made if we are to keep the competition healthy while encouraging all possible kinds of experiment and development. Framing these rules is a difficult technical problem in which it is easy to be restrictive but difficult to be permissive. The main value of the race derives from technical permissiveness.

Many points of design will emerge from a study of this book but I hope that one in particular will sink home with future competitors: six masts went over the side in conditions that do not seem to have been in any way extreme. Dismasting in this way is absurd and unnecessary and could easily be eliminated.

Frank Page of *The Observer* was the right person to write this account, having been actively involved in the 1972 race from its early planning through to its finish. He has also put in some good research on the earlier races, and the result is a book that is very well worth reading.

H G HASLER

Curdridge, August 1972

Introduction

When people ask me what I do for a living and learn that I write about motor cars and boats for *The Observer*, they are often moved to make envious noises. It is a rewarding combination, of course, and I am in no hurry to pass it on to anyone else. But like all jobs, it has its delights and its drudgeries. Working on the 1972 Observer Singlehanded Race was almost all delight.

I was lucky enough to meet a large number of very stimulating people; to study some of the most fascinating boats ever built; to share in some of the most dramatic adventures in the history of the Observer race; and above all to make a host of new friends.

I hope this book will convey the excitement and enjoyment I found in all this. Certainly it should record my debt to the many who made it possible for me to report the race and write the book. To David Astor, Clifford Makins, Donald Trelford, Ken Obank, and Gary Woodhouse at *The Observer*. To Blondie Hasler for his enormous encouragement and encyclopaedic authority about the race. To Jack Odling-Smee and Terence Shaw of the Royal Western Yacht Club of England, and their respective wives, Nancy and Ruth. To Liz Balcon, Shirley Smith, and Brian Beaumont-Nesbit of *The Observer*'s promotions department, who told me all the important things I should have known and didn't. To Shirley Clifford, who was their efficient stand-in in Newport. To Peter Dunning and all his team at the Port O'Call Marina. To all the many people in America who made me welcome – Gerry and Dottie Nevins, Murray and Barbara Davis, Bill and Lois Muessel, and so many more. And to Bill and Mary Thomas, and Dr Robin Wallace of the Ida Lewis Yacht Club.

But most of all I must thank the competitors. Without exception they were generous with their help, information, and time. I only hope I have done them as well as they deserve. This book was completed after I heard that Sir Francis Chichester had died. I hope it may serve as a small memorial to a great sailor and gallant adventurer.

Like all sport, sailing is a very effective way of breaking down barriers of country, creed, or class. Those 55 solo sailors who sailed from Plymouth on 17 June 1972 represent a very wide cross-section of the world, and anyone who was privileged to meet and mix with them as I was must derive a deeper understanding of his fellow men as a result. I only hope I can again be on the scene the next time a bunch of singlehanders decides to go solo to America.

Forethought

I must go down to the seas again, to the lonely sea and the sky,
And all I ask is a tall ship and a star to steer her by,
And the wheel's kick and the wind's song and the white sail's shaking,
And the grey mist in the sea's face and a grey dawn breaking.

I must go down to the seas again, for the call of the running tide
Is a wild call and a clear call that cannot be denied;
And all I ask is a windy day with the white clouds flying,
And the flung spray and the blown spume, and the sea gulls crying.

I must go down to the seas again, to the vagrant gypsy life,
To the gull's way and the whale's way where the wind's like a whetted knife;
And all I ask is a merry yarn from a laughing fellow rover,
And quiet sleep and a sweet dream when the long trick's over.

John Masefield *Salt Water Ballads*

1   The Reason Why

Why do men – and some women – choose to sail alone on the ocean? Is it for the temporal rewards like public recognition and the opportunities to make money that go with fame? Or is it to satisfy more spiritual appetites – a natural taste for adventure, a need for a sense of achievement, a desire to cleanse the soul by an escape from the pressures of our society, or a craving for the inner peace that comes to a man who has amassed some evidence to support the fragile thesis that he is master of his own fate?

Inevitably, there are as many combinations of these factors as there are singlehanded sailors. The most commercially minded solo yachtsman would find it difficult to face the rigours of an ocean passage alone without some degree of relish for adventure. On the other hand, the most retiring and spiritual of those who wander the oceans of the world unaided seem occasionally to welcome the limelight of a press interview or the opportunity to recount in a book the most testing adventures of their voyages.

Look at the most famous singlehanded sailor of them all, Sir Francis Chichester. He helped to start the Observer Singlehanded, back in the late fifties, then won the first race (in 1960) at the helm of *Gipsy Moth III*. It brought him back into the public eye after a gap of 30 years since his equally adventurous solo flying exploits in the twenties.

And he obviously enjoyed it. After writing his book about the first race, he set off again for America alone to set a faster time, then sailed in second to Eric Tabarly in the 1964 Observer race. Those voyages paved the way to his great circumnavigation, his knighthood, and his public acclaim by millions. Yet he still goes on finding new adventures. What prompts him to set himself ever more difficult targets at a time in life when most men are content with the security of a corner armchair and a television set? An appetite for fame is undoubtedly part of it, and fame for Sir Francis means healthy contracts for books, television appearances, and so on.

But it's not just fame that is the spur. Chichester is a natural adventurer. It makes him happy to meet the challenge of sailing unaided the sort of boat which would normally need a crew of eight. Not just cruising it across the ocean either; actually racing it every yard of the way. And facing that challenge will only bring him real happiness if he does it alone. In his book *Alone Across the Atlantic*, which he wrote after the triumph of the 1960 Singlehanded, he says 'Somehow, I never seemed to enjoy so much doing things with other people. I know I don't do a thing nearly as well when with someone. It makes me think I was cut out for solo jobs, and any attempt to diverge from that lot only makes me a half-person. It looks as though the only way to be happy is to do fully what you are destined for.'

As a contrast, consider the recluse of the singlehanded sailors, Bernard Moitessier. This lonely Frenchman would almost certainly have been first home in the *Sunday Times* round-the-world singlehanded race of 1968-9, but chose to by-pass the adulation of the waiting crowds and sail on into the Indian Ocean to his personal peace and tranquillity. A spiritual man no doubt, but even though he disdains money and actually gave away the royalties of his book *The Long Way*, the fact is that he felt he had to write a book – there had to be some connection.

But amidst all the blends of motives that send the solo sailors down to the seas again, one factor is always there – courage. For to sail alone on any stretch of open water is to face the challenge of the unpredictable sea and sky. Make no mistake, the sea's menaces can never be foretold with certainty. Even the most experienced seaman knows that he can never rely on the constancy of the elements. You can stuff your boat with charts and pilot books, listen to every radio weather forecast for shipping, study the clouds and currents every hour of the day and still be surprised by a freak squall, a bank of dense fog, a sudden absence of wind, or the chilling sight of a threatening iceberg.

And for the singlehander, not all the dangers are natural ones. He must eat and sleep sometime, so he has to live with the threat of some disaster striking while he is below deck. He risks being run down while he is asleep, or of running down some other craft while he is not on watch. When solo sailors seldom went to sea in boats more than 30 feet in length, this was scarcely a problem. They were likely to come off worst in any collision and it was a risk they had to be prepared to take. But in the last few years both the size and power of yachts for single-handers have increased enormously. Nowadays the steel hull of a boat like Chay Blyth's 59 foot ketch *British Steel* could slice into a fishing boat with dire results – perhaps even sending it to the bottom.

In addition, the singlehander has to rely greatly on what is really his 'crew' – the self-steering gear. If it functions well, he can leave it in charge while he changes sail, trims for maximum speed, checks his position, writes his log, catches up on food and rest. If it doesn't function properly, all sorts of problems can arise. Incorrect operation can send the boat on a wrong course – perhaps towards danger. Total non-function means the sailor must man the helm for much of the time and somehow fit in all those routine tasks as well. It is not an impossible task – Robin Knox-Johnston managed it for a large proportion of his first nonstop solo sail round the world in *Suhaili* – but it does intensify enormously the physical demands made on the sailor.

It takes courage, too, to go willingly out of reach of help in adversity. To face, totally unaided, all the possibilities of disaster that can strike the solo sailor. And that means not only the kind of disaster that can result from bad weather, but also the sort of casual accident that would be a minor alarm at home but could easily be fatal when the nearest help is hundreds of miles away. The singlehander accepts that his boat might suffer a knockdown, even a cap-size. That's the kind of risk he knows he has to accept. But how can you prepare yourself for the freak accident, such as being holed by a whale, getting a bout of food poisoning, breaking a leg through being tossed about the boat in a storm, or gashing open a limb on a piece of gear torn from its mounting by the force of the wind?

The lone sailor accepts that any of these things is possible and that each of them could be final, because even with high power transmitters pumping out distress calls, there is a heavy weight of odds against rescue. For all the shipping on the seas, a small boat off the main shipping lanes stands little chance of rapid discovery and aid, even if the call is heard. And in certain areas of the world – the Southern Ocean, for example – hopes of help from boat or airplane are virtually non-existent. It is difficult enough trying to locate a singlehanded yachtsman rounding Cape Horn, say, with constant radio communication and land only a few miles away. Several days' sailing out into the ocean, it becomes nearly impossible. The sea is still a very big place. Which is why it can also be a very lonely place.

Yet being alone seems to put an extra edge on the sharpness of the adventure for those who relish singlehanded sailing. And maybe that is because sailing alone is really the last adventurous activity that gives scope for sustained endeavour completely independent of any other person. Perhaps the closest parallels are the lone explorer or the trapper in the frozen wastes. They can certainly find adventure alone, but how long can they survive without returning to base for fresh supplies? Three months maybe? I doubt more. Yet the singlehanded sailor can cruise the oceans of the world for a year or more if he chooses, augmenting his original supplies with water from the skies and fish from the sea, while harnessing the wind as his motive power.

Other individualists are even more dependent upon sustenance by others. A mountaineer can scale the lesser heights alone, but for an assault on a major peak he must have the support of backup climbers and porters. The racing driver cannot compete with-out his mechanics and pit staff. The most spectacular adventurers of our time – the men who first trod the surface of the moon – needed the biggest support team of all to make their exploits possible.

Perhaps the nearest parallel to sailing is the chal-lenge of the mountains. H W Tilman, a dedicated adventurer and an expert climber and seaman, writes in his book *Mischief in Patagonia*: 'There is something in common between the arts of sailing and climbing. Each is intimately concerned with essential things, which from time to time demand from men who practise those arts whatever self-reliance, prudence, and endurance they may have. The sea and the hills offer challenges to those who venture upon them, and in the acceptance of these, and in the meeting of them as best he can, lies the sailor's or the mountain-eer's reward. An essential difference is, perhaps, that the mountaineer usually accepts the challenge on his own terms, whereas once at sea the sailor has no say in the matter and in consequence may suffer more often the salutary and humbling emotion of fear.'

Since this book is about the art of solo sailing in

general and the Observer Singlehanded race to America in particular, it is important to point out here that not all the singlehanders who want to enter the Observer race are dedicated solo men. Indeed, not all the men who have done epic long-distance voyages alone are singlehanders by natural inclination. Robin Knox-Johnston has not sailed any distance on his own since he returned triumphantly to Falmouth after his circumnavigation. He faced that great challenge for other reasons than the lure of lone adventure.

In this he is quite different from the obvious loners like Chichester and Sir Alec Rose. And so are many of the people who have competed in the Observer race since it was first sailed in 1960. Geoffrey Williams, for example, who won the 1968 race in *Sir Thomas Lipton*, has scarcely sailed alone since, and many of the entrants for the 1972 race admit quite openly that the only reason they take on the solo trip is because it is part of the rules. Brian Cooke, who sailed *British Steel* in this year's race, told me that he enjoyed sailing alone but would not do a lot of it if it were not as preparation for the Observer Singlehanded. 'I don't do it because I want to get away from people, and I wouldn't like to do it all the time,' he said. 'A number of times during the 1968 race when there was a wonderful sunset I felt I would have liked to share it with other shipmates. But I thoroughly enjoyed the last race and I was very sorry when the wonderful experience was coming to an end. Indeed I must admit to a very slight resentment that my privacy was shattered at the end.'

Here Cooke expresses a sentiment that is echoed by many of the long-distance singlehanders who would repudiate any description of themselves as true loners. Robin Knox-Johnston told me that a fortnight from home he was feeling very unsettled that it was going to end, and Chay Blyth quotes entries from his log in his book *The Impossible Voyage* about being troubled by dreams near the end of his round-the-world sail. 'Is something wrong to produce these feelings and thoughts? Could it be that I know I'll soon be in contact with people again and it's having an effect? Could it be that the voyage is almost over, and I'm subconsciously digging my heels in so as to prolong the trip? But this doesn't seem right because of my attitude to get home within 300 days.'

It seems there is something catching about sailing alone. For women as well as men. I asked Nicolette

Milnes Walker if she had contracted the singlehanded 'bug' during her solo sail to America in 1971. 'No, I don't think I did,' she said. 'But I do have mixed feelings about it and I would like to do a longer voyage to get them straight. Six weeks, the time I took to get to Newport, is too short. It takes about three weeks to get used to being alone and by that time you're getting to the other side. A singlehanded sail should either be a week or four or five months.'

Mrs Coward, as Nicolette now is, makes a very good example of the singlehanded adventurer who is totally frank about her motivations – perhaps only to be expected from a trained psychologist. She admits that one of the results from her voyage that gives her enormous pleasure is the fame it has brought her. 'It is very attractive to have public recognition,' she told me. 'But it was much more public than I expected. If I had known all that I wouldn't have gone. All those dinners and speeches – it's pretty appalling. But it is marvellous to be famous; to see your name in the *Guinness Book of Records*. You know, you think to yourself "People can go faster and so on, but to be first, that's the thing."'

She is also quite unabashed at saying she needed publicity to make her trip commercially viable. As the first woman to cross the Atlantic nonstop and alone (Ann Davison did it by way of the Azores in the early fifties) she was very much aware of her news value – and this has paid off in terms of television and newspaper interviews, talks to clubs and other organisations, while at the same time arousing interest in her book. But if that sounds blatantly commercial, it must be balanced against the equally realistic way Nicolette sums up the other benefits she derived from the solo sail.

'I have become a different person,' she said. 'It has given me much more selfconfidence, and I have got this obsession out of my system. Of course people ask me if I am going to sail round the world next. I confess to a sneaking desire to do it, but I won't, because I don't want to get hooked on being a professional adventurer. I am looking for a different quality of adventure. The adventure of writing my book, for example, meeting the Queen and the Prime Minister, driving in a rally – these are my adventures now. Especially writing, because it's a thing that you can go on getting better and better at.'

So, in that solo sailor there is a blend of hard-headed commercialism with a concerned realism about the dangers of being too 'professional'. And it is still tinged with a sentiment that no singlehander would be ashamed of. 'I like to do things entirely on my own responsibility – so that all the credit is mine and all the failure is mine too.'

One of the men who would undoubtedly echo those sentiments is Bill Howell, the Australian dentist who lives and works in London. The 1972 Observer Singlehanded was his third in a row. He is probably the best blend of all the motivations for sailing singlehanded that you could find. Though he sailed in 1968 as a sponsored boat – his catamaran was named *Golden Cockerel* because that is the symbol of the Courage brewery that helped him to equip it – he did not ask for a sponsor's help a second time. Though he carried a radio and reported to the *Daily Mail* in 1968, for 1972 he refused offers of cash from newspapers so that he could remove the radio to lighten the boat and thus make it more competitive.

So although he welcomed commercial support when it was essential, he also relished being entirely self-sufficient when that was possible. He, too, is a great believer in doing things entirely on his own responsibility. Indeed, he thinks this is one of the basic rewards of sailing solo. 'It's the excitement of taking a risk – but a calculated risk. You prepare the boat and everything is done by yourself. We need to take a risk to discover ourselves, and sailing alone fulfils that need. It makes you a better person. You sit down for months figuring out what you are going to do, so you've prepared yourself against all possibilities. Every male needs some sort of danger – it goes back to the days when man was a hunter. He developed a sort of hunger for adventure. And if you love adventure, whatever you do is much more adventurous if you do it alone. So your sense of achievement is also all the greater. When you've faced a problem and solved it you feel ten feet high.'

Howell also derives another benefit from solo sailing which is not always shared by others. He finds it sharpens his reflexes, both physical and mental. Handling a boat alone tunes the body very quickly, but the less familiar result is the effect on the mind. Howell says, 'Nobody is normally totally alone for the length of time we are on the Transatlantic Race. After about five days at sea you find your mind becomes much sharper than it is when you are on

land. I find I can read a book on anatomy, say, and where I would take 20 minutes to read a page at home, out there I can take it in at one reading – three or four minutes. And, you know, it's a sort of religious thing – like the old prophets going out into the wilderness for 40 days. Jesus Christ did it.'

That sounds very logical, yet Nicolette Coward's experience was almost the opposite. She admits that she became very idle during her transatlantic sail. 'My mind seemed to slow down a lot and become less original. The entries in my log for the first few weeks are much more interesting than later on.'

But these become effects of solo sailing rather than causes. There are other characteristics of singlehanded sailors that need to be examined. And these are the traits of the true loner, the men who find complete fulfilment in being alone on the ocean with no other end in mind. Publicity and fame mean almost nothing to them; monetary reward is unimportant because all they need are a few basic supplies whenever they choose to cease wandering for a few days; they are not concerned about getting from one point to another in any special time or by any special route. They are the gypsies of the oceans.

Perhaps Bernard Moitessier is the supreme example of this type, but there are also some British yachtsmen who fit into the category – though any one of them would rebel at being categorised! One of the best examples among Englishmen is Sir Alec Rose, who sailed his *Lively Lady* to Newport in the 1964 Observer Singlehanded and later circumnavigated the world – at his own pace and for his own delight.

Sir Alec wrote an illuminating feature for the American yachting journal *Sail* early in 1972. In it he said, 'I find sailing alone, offshore and off the main shipping lanes, particularly enjoyable. There is a wonderful feeling of contentment and of being self-sufficient when at sea and out of touch with one's fellow human beings.

'But why, people ask, alone? I know why but it is difficult to put into words. To start with, a man must be basically of a certain type – a sort of "dark horse" if you like, a thinker, a dreamer, an idealist and individualist. A man prepared to stand on his own feet or fall by his own decisions . . . These are not often antisocial people. Indeed, they are usually good company. But according to their sense of values money, though essential to achieve their

4

ambitions, is not in itself important.' For a man who finds it hard to put his thoughts into words, Sir Alec makes light of his difficulties. He captures the flavour of the confirmed singlehander very well.

The man who actually originated the Observer Singlehanded back in the late fifties is also a dedicated lone sailor. Colonel H G (Blondie) Hasler devised the race and then sailed in the 1960 and 1964 events. He took his little Folkboat *Jester* into second place behind Francis Chichester in 1960 and finished fifth (just behind Rose) four years later.

He says 'The only pleasure I get at sea really is becoming isolated. I get a tremendous pleasure out of existing in a world that only goes as far as the horizon. I shrink from contact. I have never had a wireless receiver yet in a transatlantic race for this reason. And the result of that is that I give myself quite unnecessary problems on longitude – in the last race I was something over 30 miles out on longitude both going to America and coming back, because I wouldn't carry a receiver and relied on deck watches. But this so happens to make me feel good – I feel as though I have really done something by myself. I love being completely independent.'

Hasler often talks about 'our forefathers' and expresses his intense admiration for the great sailors of earlier centuries who first charted unknown coasts and crossed unknown oceans. He talks, too, of being 'contaminated' by his friend Peter Hamilton, who believes in taking the minimum of navigational aids when going sailing (Hamilton once sailed up the east coast of England with just an AA handbook for a chart).

'It is the only way you can attempt to recapture or understand the astonishing skills of our forefathers,' says Hasler. 'One's mind just boggles at the seamanship of the people who went out and explored the world in ships which were grossly incapable of good sailing. To avoid shipwreck and still to explore an unknown coast was a fantastic piece of seamanship.

'Peter Hamilton, on his honeymoon, started off across the Pacific with his new wife, who had never really sailed before. He allowed himself one chart of the entire Pacific and the Admiralty pilot books. Of course, none of the small islands were even marked on his chart but he used to read the book and say, "This sounds rather good. Here's an island called something which is said to be latitude this and

longitude that – let's go there." And they would draw a kind of rough chart of the island from the sailing directions and then go to the island and see how well they had done it. This to me would be fascinating. I can understand how much more fun it would be to a good seaman than with thirty quid's worth of charts, wireless, and everything else.'

The fascination of the Pacific Ocean stills calls to Bill Howell at times, too. He thinks of it as the only real place for the true lone sailor to roam the seas. 'Look at Slocum and those who sailed so much in the Pacific,' he says, 'they were never racing. The real singlehanded sailor is not competitive. And of course, that's the place to be – not this lousy Atlantic Ocean – that's where the islands are. That's where the lotus eating is. And that's where you can find your own peace. I remember when I did my longest voyage in the Pacific – from Honolulu to British Columbia. When I got there I didn't want to go ashore. I just dropped the hook and settled down to read a couple of books. I sat aboard and read for about 24 hours.'

It's not difficult to imagine a man who had garnered such serenity from his sailing echoing the feelings expressed in the poetical words of Val Howells, the Welshman who competed in the first two Observer races – the 'black-bearded Viking' as Francis Chichester called him. With a feeling for words spoken with a Welsh lilt that Dylan Thomas would have relished, Howells once expressed his own philosophy of the sea in a radio talk which, thankfully, has been perpetuated on a BBC record called *Sea and Sail*.

'You may not believe it, but I'm usually relieved to leave the land behind. A boat's not something that's meant to swing around a mooring in a muddy creek. A boat's meant to take you away from the land. But why so far from land? Why across 3,000 miles of ocean? And why alone? Well, isn't there a bit of the maverick, the rogue animal, in all of us? What's the point of running with the herd all the time – conforming, consenting, keeping in the fashion, keeping in the groove? Must we all be the same? If you spend all your life trying to keep up with the Joneses all you learn in the end is that the Joneses are very boring people. And you come to look like them and then it's too late to change. Not for me, thanks. I think you've got to work at being yourself, at getting to know yourself, warts and all

5

... You see yourself in a strange, at least an unfamiliar perspective ... When you've tended your boat every yard of the way; when you've done a thousand miles in her and every creak and shudder is familiar; when you know every angle she can show you to the sea and sky, you begin to husband the wind as though by second nature. If the wind changes its key by so much as a semitone, it brings you from below to change your sail. You don't have to think about it. You can settle now to the rhythms of the ocean.

'And as the days go by you begin to have time to look into yourself ... Surrounded by sea and nothing but sea, with nothing to focus on but yourself, you weigh yourself up ... Whatever hunger it is that drives a man away alone, there's a limit to it. There's a limit to lying on your 12 ton floating psychiatrist's couch. The truth is, the crossing of an ocean alone in a small boat doesn't leave you with a feeling of achievement that will allow you to sit back and muse about it endlessly until your beard is altogether white.

'The sea is all persuasion and promises. It'll tease you back and promise you peace again – or what passes for peace. It creates as many desires as it satisfies – and it leaves you less uppity ... Three thousand miles alone. It's a long way to prove such a simple truth. Too far to go? I believe every man can be his own artist. I don't really think you need to have a brush to be an artist. By an artist I mean a man with a freshness of eye, living on distances, though they are close about him. Living, if you like, on the horizon of himself.'

On the horizon of himself. An indulgent phrase perhaps, but it captures much of what the singlehanders derive from their solitary sport. Remember Blondie Hasler's 'world that only goes as far as the horizon'. And also the words of another Observer Singlehanded pioneer – Dr David Lewis, the New Zealand-born solo sailor who competed in the 1960 and 1964 races. Then he journeyed across the Pacific with his wife and two small children aboard the catamaran *Rehu Moana*, and wrote later about his children, 'I hope they will grow up to face life in this same spirit; that they will feel the discontent that makes living for the daily round not enough, so that they, too, will need to sail beyond their own sunsets.'

There remains one motivation which seems to affect few singlehanders overtly but which may be an underlying current in many of them – patriotism. The most obvious example is Robin Knox-Johnston, who admits quite freely that one of the main reasons why he took on the solo circumnavigation was to do it for Britain. 'Once Chichester and Rose had shown that this trip was possible I could not accept that anyone but a Briton should be the first to do it, and I wanted to be that Briton,' he writes in his book *A World Of My Own*.

It is the kind of patriotism that borders on chauvinism, and which one expects to find in the French more than the English these days. Indeed, it was some particularly chauvinistic writing in *Paris-Match* that really stirred up Knox-Johnston to make preparations for a round-the-world nonstop sail. He read there the eulogies for Eric Tabarly's victory in the 1964 Observer Singlehanded. ' "Frenchman supreme on the Anglo-Saxon Ocean," *Paris-Match* had screamed, the inference being that the Island Race had been proved inferior seamen to the French. This had made my blood boil at the time and I could picture the headlines if Tabarly became the first person to sail right round the world nonstop. We'd never hear the last of it.'

That was how Knox-Johnston wrote about the situation in his book. And the blood still has a low boiling point. I spoke to him a few months before the 1972 Observer race and the patriotism was still pumping uninhibitedly through his veins. 'I feel very strongly about this,' he said. 'We've gone through a phase now for about ten years when people seem to take a delight in being beaten and apologising for things – they're masochists. It infuriates me. We've nothing to be ashamed of in this country.'

From an armchair table-thumper this might sound empty invective. But from a man who has actually done what he set out to do for his country – despite enormous setbacks such as polluted water tanks, nonfunctioning radio, disintegrated self-steering gear, collapsed main boom, sheered tiller and leaking hull – it has an impressive conviction.

So we have run the gamut of all the reasons that lone sailors will admit to for staking their lives against the elements in the middle of an unfriendly sea. Fame and fortune; adventure and self-discovery; to sharpen the mind and recreate the endeavours of our forbears; to eat the lotus and escape the Joneses, and to wave the flag for Queen and country. Stated

6

so bluntly, it seems an odd collection of motivations, no matter how they are balanced out in the individual.

But perhaps there is a deeper, subconscious urge that is the common ground on which all these aspirations to adventure are built. That is man's constant need to feel that he is more than a mere pawn in the hands of some overwhelming Fate; to prove to himself that he can ride the whirlwind and escape unscathed. Psychologists tell us that this is a basic motivation in the motor racing driver – he flirts with death to prove he is master of his own destiny. And the crowds flock to the race tracks to see one of their number balance on the edge of death and come back to the living triumphant. If an ace dies in a crash, the crowd is saddened and dull. If he cartwheels along the track, then emerges from the wreckage battered but still able to wave, the crowd exults.

So the rest of us who watch the exploits of the singlehanders from afar try to experience vicariously their experience of facing up to the steep odds of nature and coming safely home again. Remember the huge crowds at Plymouth, Falmouth, and the Hamble for the triumphant returns of Chichester, Knox-Johnston, and Blyth? Wasn't every one of those cheering, waving onlookers trying to sing, with their heroes, the song of the man who has come through?

It is an astonishing scene to witness – one small boat in a huge armada of welcoming craft and vast crowds thronging the waterside. Robert Manry, the quiet American journalist who crossed the Atlantic alone in a tiny 13½ foot boat called *Tinkerbelle*, in 1965, was certainly astonished at his reception when he arrived in Falmouth. He expected to slip in, tie up somewhere and creep off to a hotel to catch up on sleep. But he reckoned without the thousands who had heard about his voyage in a boat so small he could not even lie down to sleep; the crowds who wanted to see the man who dared to affront the ocean and the heavens and get away with it.

Manry, too, wrote a book. And perhaps because he was a writer by profession he came nearest to summing up in a few sentences all the interwoven needs and urges that make the solo sailor set out across the seas. 'The voyage was something I simply *had* to do, had wanted to do for a long, long time,' he wrote in *Tinkerbelle*. 'I think probably the most important thing it had done for me was to enable me to stand back, away from human society ashore, and look at life for a little while from a new perspective. The Atlantic Ocean had not been a place for trivialities, and I think, perhaps, that fact may have done something to make me a better person inside than I had been before.

'Anyway, I hope it did . . . Though the wind and sea were sometimes my adversaries, they were mostly friendly and they behaved with straightforward honesty according to their inherent natures. To know them was to respect them.

'I must confess that, seen from the peace and quiet of mid-ocean, many aspects of life on land seem grim indeed. I couldn't help thinking of the grey-flannel suit brigades in the big cities ashore living in a kind of lock-step frenzy, battling noisy highways or subway traffic to get to work in the morning and to return home in the evening, existing on pure nervous energy in between, having to be alert to opportunities to get ahead and on guard against the encroachment of rivals.'

That is why the solo sailors go to sea. To prove to others that they are different from the Joneses, the grey-flannel suit brigades, the conformers; and to prove to themselves that they can face the challenge of the oceans and return to harbour triumphant.

2 A Century of Singlehanding

Who can tell when a man first felt the urge to sail off alone to find his own horizon? Maybe it was before what we call civilisation had blossomed in Europe, for the Polynesians of the South Pacific were experts at sailing and boat construction long before the Egyptians, Greeks, and Phoenecians did their first tentative coast-hugging in the Mediterranean. The Egyptians invented the rudder and were among the first to use sails, but they seldom adventured beyond the Nile Delta. About the same time, on the other side of the world, the Polynesians were traversing the vast expanses of the South Pacific in sleek and speedy proas by a kind of intuitive navigation.

Perhaps one of them was the first to rebel against the tribal instinct and go it alone. Perhaps not. There is no easy reference point for the start of long-distance singlehanding, because the records are thin and opinions vary as to what is long-distance when you are alone in a boat. But one classic voyage must set the standard – the trans-Atlantic passage. And as far as we know, all the solo crossings of that ocean have been in the last hundred years.

Appropriately enough, the first boat to carry a solo sailor across the Western Ocean was called *Centennial*. She was a 20 foot dory rigged as a gaff cutter and her crew was a young Banks fisherman called Alfred Johnson. The year was 1876 and the reason given for the voyage, and for the name of the boat, was that 1876 marked the hundredth anniversary of the United States of America. He made the crossing in 64 days, arriving in Abercastle, Pembrokeshire, after a voyage that included being capsized in a gale and four days of rain and fog without any means of drying clothes or heating food. Johnson was undoubtedly a very tough seaman, and his exploit is all the more remarkable for the fact that he had little knowledge of navigation and relied largely upon passing ships to find out his position.

An impressive start to the history of singlehanding across the Atlantic, yet the next chapter in the story is even more amazing. In 1891 there was the first ever singlehanded race across. It was the result of a challenge by Si Lawlor, an American small boat sailor, to William Andrews, a piano maker with an evident relish for voyages of endurance. Andrews had already crossed the Atlantic in a small boat, the *Nautilus*, with his younger brother Walter in the year 1878. Ten years later he set out to sail to Europe alone but had to give up half way across because his boat *Dark Secret* was not as seaworthy as *Nautilus* had been.

Nothing daunted, he planned another single-handed crossing for 1891. Lawlor heard about it and decided to go at the same time in a similar size craft. So in June 1891 two frighteningly small boats set out to race across the Atlantic. They were only 15 feet long overall with a 5 foot beam. Andrews' boat was called *Mermaid*, Lawlor's *Sea Serpent*.

For Andrews, it was another disaster. *Mermaid* capsized in mid-ocean two months after the start and he was lucky to be picked up, exhausted, by the steamer *Ebruz*. Meanwhile Lawlor had already arrived in Coverack, Cornwall (not far from the Lizard), after crossing in the incredible time of 45 days. *Sea Serpent* had twice been on her beam ends and Lawlor had also had to frighten off a shark with an explosive yacht salute, so it was far from an uneventful voyage. Nevertheless it set a pace which is not easy to match even in a modern yacht of much greater length.

William Andrews eventually fulfilled his ambition to sail across alone. He made it the next year in a boat only 14 feet 6 inches long, by way of the Azores. But it took 84 days. He eventually decided at the age of 61 to make a fifth attempt to sail across, this time with his wife. They were sighted a week out, heading into a heavy gale – and oblivion.

In the late nineteenth century it seemed to be a matter of pride among these singlehanders to put to sea in the smallest possible boat. But there were exceptions. The most notable is Captain Rudolph Frietsch, a Finn who set out from New York in 1894 at the helm of a 40 foot schooner called *Nina*. He arrived at Queenstown in Ireland in 35 days, averaging a reasonable 80 miles a day.

Information about these early solo passages is hard to come by, but fortunately we have an excellent record of the most significant singlehanded sail in the nineteenth century. It is *Sailing Alone Around the World*, the enchanting book written by Captain Joshua Slocum, who can rightly be called the father of singlehanded sailing.

He describes not only his transatlantic voyage, but also his complete circumnavigation, which started from Boston in April 1895 and ended there just over three years later. The book is a classic, which nobody interested in singlehanded sailing should ignore. It is enough here to record that Slocum spent much of the voyage with the helm lashed and *Spray* making her own way at her own speed. Their voyage lay across the Western Ocean to Gibraltar, then down the Atlantic to the west coast of South America and the Magellan Strait, through the Pacific by way of many of the islands to Australia and the Torres Strait, across the Indian Ocean and round the Cape of Good Hope into the long home run up the Atlantic to Boston by way of the West Indies. Slocum's was no record-breaking dash; it was a voyage of self-discovery and contemplation.

He set off with a library of 500 books and he spent many hours reading – a common pastime among singlehanders. Robin Knox-Johnston took all the classics he had meant to read but never got down to when he went round the world. Blondie Hasler took a year's supply of *New Yorker* magazines on the first Observer Singlehanded race and read them one by one. By contrast, Chay Blyth had a minimum library for his round-the-world sail. He is a man of action rather than words.

Slocum had plenty to contemplate on his journey. When he set out he was 51 and had spent much of his life on the sea. Bald and thin, this tough Nova Scotian had always been a good sailor, starting as a lad 'before the mast' and working up to command a clipper ship by the age of 26. In the 1880s he was captain and part-owner of the *Northern Light*, then the finest American sailing vessel afloat, and later owned and sailed the bark *Aquidneck*. It was on this ship that he quelled a mutiny, killing two of his cut-throat crew to do so, and experienced a shipwreck off the coast of Brazil. Stranded there, he built a 35 foot 'canoe' with Chinese lugsails and sailed his wife and sons back to America.

But by the nineties his fortunes were fading. The sailing ship trade was wilting and there were no positions for captains. So he built the *Spray*, using some parts remaining from an old boat of the same name, and set out around the world. He crossed from Yarmouth, Nova Scotia, to Fayal in the Azores in 22 days, then after a rest continued to Gibraltar in another 11 days. It was the start of a great adventure brilliantly perpetuated in the book.

The *Spray* was not an ocean greyhound by any means. She was 37 foot long, 15 foot in the beam, and her best speed was about eight knots. But she was sturdily built – as she needed to be to carry Captain Slocum through some of his adventures – and she could stir her crew to some of the best descriptive writing about sailing that has ever been printed. Just sample the joy of the open water that Slocum breathes into this short passage about his first day on a voyage that was to last over three years.

'*Spray* rounded Deer Island Light at the rate of seven knots. Passing it she squared away direct for Gloucester to procure there some fishermen's stores. Waves dancing joyously across Massachusetts Bay met her coming out of the harbour to dash them into myriads of sparkling gems that hung about her at every surge. The day was perfect, the sunlight clear and strong. Every particle of water thrown into the air became a gem, and the *Spray*, bounding ahead, snatched necklace after necklace from the sea, and as often threw them away. We have all seen miniature rainbows about a ship's prow, but the *Spray* flung out a bow of her own that day, such as I had never seen before. Her good angel had embarked on the voyage; I so read it in the sea.'

Slocum's book was published in 1900. Maybe that had much to do with the ever-increasing number of singlehanded sailors who crossed the oceans in the early part of the twentieth century.

Captain Tom Drake was another solo sailor in the Slocum mould. He too first went to sea as a lad – in a fishing sloop out of Grimsby. He was born an Englishman in 1863 but adopted America as his country after many years sailing around the world in square-riggers. Then he decided that the only companions he wanted for a happy life were a small schooner and the sea. So he built his own ideal boat to his own eclectic design and called it *Sir Francis*.

Together they sailed for many years in the Pacific, off the coast of South America, and in the Caribbean, until *Sir Francis* was forced ashore near Port Angel, Oaxaca. After a lucky escape from Pancho Villa's desperadoes, Drake soon built himself another boat and set off on more lone voyagings. His most famous craft was *Pilgrim*, a double-ender of 35 feet overall, which carried him the length of the coastlines of the Americas before he sailed across the Atlantic from Charleston, South Carolina. It was a good passage, past the Azores and on to the English Channel, where a gale forced Drake to beat about off Cornwall for nearly a week before he was able to put into Fowey after a voyage of 52 days.

Those who met him in port found Drake a warm and friendly man, always ready to talk. Yet at heart there seemed to be a profound loneliness that made him always itch to wander the waters of the world. 'It isn't,' he said, 'that life ashore is distasteful to me. But life at sea is better.' Later he wrote to a friend, 'I don't suppose many of you can understand this craving of mine for blue water, but you get mighty close to something big when you're alone at sea. At times I am lonely all right, but probably no more than an albatross or the North Star.'

Drake lost *Pilgrim* in 1929 when she was forced ashore near the Hook of Holland in a fierce gale while he was sailing back from Scandinavian waters to France. She had logged nearly 30,000 miles and called at 117 ports in four years of cruising round the world. Undeterred, the 66-year-old skipper went back to the United States and started to build yet another boat to his own design.

He knew nothing of the professional yacht designer's rules, coefficients, and formulae, yet his yachts were always strong and seaworthy. He said that when he wanted to build a boat he first pictured her in his mind for a while, then made a model and finally got on with the job of actual building. And it worked. His last boat, *Progress*, rode out a 90-mile-an-hour gale in the Pacific even though the heavy seas had smashed her bowsprit, carried away the triple-reefed mainsail and storm jib, and damaged her rigging. Drake broke his right arm in the storm, but later said philosophically that he 'managed all right with my left hand'. It was, he said, the first time he had shipped water in the cockpit in 25 years.

He was then 72. A year later, in 1936, released from hospital and eager to set sail again, he refitted *Progress* and left Sausalito, California, bound single-handed for the South Seas. He was never seen or heard of again.

The same insatiable urge to roam the world affected the Frenchman Alain Gerbault. Born in 1893, he was blessed with all the talents. He became

a clever civil engineer, an international tennis player, an admired footballer, and a much-sought-after adornment to any social gathering. Yet all that had no appeal to him. He had lost many of his best friends during the first World War, when he served in the French air force, and after that he preferred his own company and escape from the pressures of organised society. 'After the war I could neither work in a city nor lead the dull life of a businessman,' he wrote. 'I wanted freedom, open air, and adventure. Early in life I became my own companion.'

So he bought the *Firecrest*, a flush-deck, gaff-rigged English cutter that had been built in Essex in 1892. She was narrow, deep, and well-balanced, measuring 39 feet overall with just 8 feet 6 inches beam. After sailing her around the Mediterranean for many months, Gerbault decided to take her across the Atlantic in 1924. They set out from Gibraltar in June 1924 and arrived in New York 101 days later, much of that time spent by Gerbault patching up the old boat's worn out rigging and sails.

In New York the *Firecrest* was refitted and re-rigged, while the owner almost casually helped France win the Davis Cup. Then they set sail again on a leisurely, contemplative circumnavigation. 'I am in no hurry,' said Gerbault, 'for I am travelling with my home and hope I shall be able to carry on always. Every man needs to find a peak, a mountain top or a remote island of his own choosing that he reaches under his own power alone in his own good time.'

But though he found many remote islands during the six years that he took to sail around the world, Gerbault never settled. He eventually sailed back into Cherbourg in July 1929, having logged more than 40,000 miles during 700 days alone at sea. But if he failed to find a resting place in which he could escape the persistent call of the sea, he did at least find a cause. In his final years he campaigned constantly for a better life for his friends in the Polynesian islands. Like Stevenson and Gauguin before him, he sensed the beauty and humility of the Polynesians – he once said that he would not want a child by a Polynesian girl because he would not wish to defile such a beautiful race. He resented their exploitation by the colonialists and protested against the laws which forbade the old Polynesian customs and dances.

But it was a vain fight, and Gerbault died of malaria in 1941 still searching for the ideal uninhabited atoll that might bring a measure of peace to his embittered old age.

Slocum, Drake, and Gerbault took plenty of time on their long voyages across the oceans. For the Argentine Vito Dumas the craving to sail alone also meant pushing on at speed to the next port. Born in 1900, this former swimming champion who took to sailing alone was obviously one of the toughest solo sailors and finest navigators in the history of singlehanding. Time and again he made nonstop ocean crossings of 7,000 miles or more; time and again he was more than 100 days at sea alone; time and again his physical strength and fine seamanship saw him through the most perilous adventures.

For 25 years he sailed alone in various parts of the world, but his peak achievement was in 1942-3 when he made a remarkably fast circumnavigation around the roaring forties in 272 days, sailing 20,420 miles with only three landfalls. This remained the fastest solo passage around the world until Francis Chichester's 24 years later.

It was a voyage that almost started with disaster. Dumas left Montevideo and sailed out into the South Atlantic into the teeth of a pampero, a 50-knot gale that had already closed the port to shipping. Two days out Dumas found that his 32 foot ketch *Lehg II* had a serious leak – a split plank in the forepeak. Making the repairs caused several cuts in his hands and soon his right arm was infected and practically useless. While the storm raged on Dumas fought to save the arm by giving himself injections.

Eventually he decided that he would have to amputate – after seven days of mounting fever and pain, something had to be done or he would die. But it was not necessary. The last day of the storm also brought a natural relief to his wounds – the poison oozed from his body and soon he was healing fast. The passage remained a stormy one, but at last, after 55 days at sea, the little *Lehg II* arrived at Cape Town.

From there Dumas sailed on three weeks later to Wellington, across the Pacific nonstop to Valparaiso in Chile and thence on to the River Plate and his home of Buenos Aires, rounding the Horn under mizzen, storm trysail, staysail, and jib. He never stayed long in a port, nor showed any relish to explore the quiet harbours and small islands of the less-frequented seas. 'One must always say goodbye to all things – ports, towns, human contacts – and pass on,' he wrote later. 'I only know that I went on again and again with a little spark glowing inside.'

It is a little spark that glowed in more and more singlehanded sailors as the years went by. By the middle of this century the legends of the loners were proliferating. There were those who built their own boats, after the tradition of Joshua Slocum. The Frenchman Marcel Bardiaux built his 30 foot sloop *Les Quatre Vents* entirely himself, spending 15,000 hours over six years on the labour of love. Then Bardiaux sailed round the world between 1950 and 1958, visiting more than 500 anchorages, and rounding Cape Horn on the way.

The Canadian John Guzzwell built his own boat, too – at the back of a fish and chip shop in Vancouver. *Trekka* was a 20 foot yawl which took Guzzwell round the world in four years.

Others preferred to buy their boats, some gleamingly new, straight from the slip; some old and rejected but restored to a seaworthy condition by weeks of hard work by their owners. The two nonstop solo circumnavigators provide a nice contrast in styles. Robin Knox-Johnston had for long nurtured ambitions to sail nonstop round the world, but all his early planning was on the basic assumption that *Suhaili* was not the boat for the job. She was too small. It was only after attempts to get sponsorship for a new and specially-designed boat had failed that Knox-Johnston resorted to using the dumpy 44 foot ketch that was originally built as a family cruiser by Indian craftsmen.

Yet *Suhaili* seldom faltered on that first solo nonstop sail around the world. She rode out some severe gales that did plenty of damage to her rigging and gear, and she also sprang a leak which had to be repaired at sea in an ingenious way that would make any solo sailor proud, but her basic structure remained sound through 313 days of sailing over 30,000 miles of ocean.

Chay Blyth, by contrast, did get his sponsorship and thus also got the boat he wanted, specially designed and brand new for the voyage. *British Steel* was designed by Robert Clark only after Chay Blyth had been promised financial support by the British Steel Corporation. And she was designed not just for singlehanding, but for the specific target of sailing round the world singlehanded against the prevailing winds and currents.

Of course, that did not mean everything went smoothly on Blyth's voyage. Indeed, he recalls in his book how after just 48 hours he made a list of seven failures of gear – mostly of not much significance, agreed, but still needing extra work by the single-hander. And he had not been at sea long before his major problem cropped up – broken poles for his big running sails. With additional worries about the strength of his mainmast, Blyth could be forgiven for not pushing on as fast as possible, but he had set out to maintain a high average speed and he kept working at it, gear failures or no.

But *British Steel* is a well balanced boat, so even when Blyth had breakages in the self-steering gear lines he was still able to keep her going well and handle sail too, and that was a major factor in his remarkable achievement of getting round the world 'against the grain' in 292 days.

Sir Francis Chichester uses a boat designed by Robert Clark, too. His latest, *Gipsy Moth V*, is not unlike *British Steel* in many ways – a ketch rigged so that the sail plan is well split up for ease of handling by one man, and with big running headsails. This is the boat in which Sir Francis attempted his trans-atlantic 'four-minute mile' – to cross 4,000 miles of ocean at an average speed of 200 miles a day. He took 22·3 days instead of 20, but that was actually 38 per cent faster than the best 4,000 mile run he had completed in *Gipsy Moth IV* during his circum-navigation in 1966–7.

Of course, the voyage around the world in *Gipsy Moth IV* – with just one stop at Sydney – is the one for which Sir Francis will always be remembered, but in one sense the less dramatic transatlantic dash is more typical of the man. Chichester seldom cruises anywhere. His personal fixation about singlehanded sailing is to plot a course and then race it – piling on every square inch of canvas the boat will take.

That's why, having narrowly failed to do 4,000 miles in 20 days, Sir Francis set off again into the North Atlantic searching for routes that would give him chances to attempt 1,000 miles in five days. Esoteric stuff? To some perhaps, but this is the kind of challenge that brings out the indomitable spirit of men like Chichester. At the end of that 1970–71 voyage *Gipsy Moth V* had been at sea for 120 days, during which she had sailed 18,581 miles – an astonishing average of 154·8 miles a day, or 1,038·9 miles a week.

It is fascinating now to recall that the name of Chichester first came back to the lips of the adventure-loving public in 1960 when plain Mr Chichester took *Gipsy Moth III* to New York in the first Observer Singlehanded race to win in what then seemed a very fast time of 40 days. This gave the restless spirit of adventure in the man a fresh boost, for it was not long after that he started planning a second transatlantic sail in *Gipsy Moth III*. In 1962 he crossed alone in 33 days – another dramatic improvement.

Then came the 1964 race, and Chichester this time getting just under his personal target of less than 30 days, though finishing second to Tabarly, and so on to the big plan – for the circumnavigation. In all this Sir Francis has proved beyond doubt that endeavour and courage are not diminished by advancing years – he was 58 at the time of the first Observer Single-handed and nearly 70 when he returned to Plymouth after the transatlantic dash, yet he was eager to go again in the 1972 race.

Sir Alec Rose is no tenderfoot either. After competing in the 1964 Observer Singlehanded race (coming fourth in 36 days) he too sailed around the world, when his age was nearly 60. His boat was the faithful 36 foot cutter *Lively Lady*; his pace the measured rhythm of the ocean, for Sir Alec has too much respect for the elements to try to dominate them. Of the 1964 race, he has written, 'The sea was boisterous and playful. I admired but respected it, acknowledging Neptune as king of the sea. Would he allow me to remain king of my sturdy yacht? Time would tell; the sea is a great leveller, and quickly humbles the big-headed sailor.'

The same humility towards the sea and sky tempered his actions during the circumnavigation. 'In parts of the voyage I was outside the reach of any help,' he wrote later. 'The Southern Ocean, particularly, was black and cold and frequented by few ships or aircraft. There, indeed, I was alone and major damage, such as dismasting, could have meant literally months of delay, possibly even failure to survive. The situation made me cautious. I took the seamanlike action of not carrying too much sail. I felt it would be better to arrive home a little later than not at all.'

Britain's two knights of circumnavigation make an interesting contrast. And there are many more solo sailors who add colour to the variegated pattern of solo sailing during this century. The solitary Englishman Edward Allcard and the courageous Norwegian Alfon Moller Hansen; the New Zealander Adrian Hayter and the Australian Fred Rebell; the intrepid little Japanese Kenichi Horie and the Swiss Michael Mermod – the list is long and valorous.

Through it all there runs a rich seam of independence of spirit. The sort of spirit that drove Ann Davison to sail the tiny *Felicity Ann* across the Atlantic even though she had been wrecked at sea and lost her husband in the wreck. The sort of self-reliance that enabled Robin Knox-Johnston to press on round the world in *Suhaili* when his boat had suffered enough gear failures to make even the keenest competitor give up in despair.

They are a formidable company, these single-handers. When you recall the highlights of their illustrious history it is hardly surprising to find so many aspiring sailors eager to join their number by competing in the classic of the solo seamen – the Observer Singlehanded race.

3 Safety and Sponsors

When the first Observer race to America was being planned in the late fifties, there was little indication that it would grow quickly into a world famous event and attract dozens of entrants to Plymouth every four years. The preliminaries were quite casual and to some extent haphazard, interspersed by a good proportion of abortive negotiations with yacht clubs and newspapers about who would organise and who sponsor the race.

But the basics remained constant. A nucleus of enthusiastic solo sailors was determined to contest a race to New York, and if no formal organisation could be fixed they would go anyway. In fact, Francis Chichester actually challenged Blondie Hasler to a race for a half-crown wager.

The most constant element in those early preparations was Blondie Hasler himself. His was the original inspiration. He wanted to hold a race that would encourage the development and efficiency of yachts and their gear. 'I wanted to have a race without handicapping formulae, the only limiting factor being what one man could do on his own,' he said later. 'The minimum of rules – I don't like rules very much.'

It is a characteristic expression of independence from a man who has always enjoyed a large measure of unorthodoxy in his life. Back in 1941, when he was a captain in the Royal Marines, he had dreamed up what seemed like a wild scheme to destroy enemy shipping in harbour. Use small boats to get up the Gironde estuary, he suggested, then you can wreak havoc actually in the harbour of Bordeaux.

It was the kind of slightly mad idea that could break down the accepted conventions of warfare when the pressure was really on, so the blond young captain was instructed to carry out his operation. He selected nine other brave and fit Marines to go with him, and together they set out to storm the fiercely-defended Bordeaux harbour in a fleet of tiny boats. They were the 'cockleshell heroes'. Eight of the ten never returned, but six enemy vessels were sunk and the raid was rated a highly successful operation.

When he left the Marines after the war as a lieutenant-colonel, Hasler developed his natural interest in experimenting – in boats, in self-steering gear, in rigs – in anything. And his compulsion for singlehanded sailing largely arose from this interest. 'I wanted to be able to sail by myself because it is extremely difficult to raise a crew who are both congenial and available to go where you want,' he said. *Jester* (Hasler's 25 foot Folkboat) was launched in 1952 and for some years Hasler experimented with a lapwing rig on her. It worked well but it was not galeproof when reefed – the wind would always get under the rolled sail and form a dangerous balloon in the canvas.

'It was while I was at this stage that I thought it would be pleasant if other people doing similar things could come along and we could have some inducement to compete with each other. It seemed that a race is always the best inducement for developing anything, and if I was getting together people aiming at ease of handling and comfort, it would have to be a demanding race, so going to windward across the North Atlantic seemed the most demanding thing to do.'

That was in 1956. The idea germinated slowly and suffered a few setbacks until 1959, when it re-gathered momentum. It was in that year that Christopher Brasher, the Olympic gold medal winning athlete who had become sports editor of *The Observer*, gave promise of sponsorship support from the newspaper. And it was in December of the same year that Hasler and Francis Chichester convinced the Royal Western Yacht Club of England that they should organise the event.

The Royal Western Yacht Club was really the obvious place for the start of the race. It has a long tradition of ocean racing (well known to offshore sailors as, among many other things, the finishing point of the classic Fastnet Race) and is ideally positioned. From Plymouth the solo sailors are quite soon out into blue water and away from the potentially hazardous crowded shipping lanes of the Channel.

The club established a Race Committee under the chairmanship of Jack Odling-Smee, a retired Army Lt-Colonel, who quickly became a wholehearted

The pioneers.
Four starters in the first Observer Singlehanded
race, back in 1960.
Left to right: Francis Chichester, Blondie Hasler,
Val Howells, and David Lewis. The French-
man Lacombe started late
Photo: Jack Esten

Eric Tabarly was hardly known in Britain before he won the second Observer Singlehanded in Pen Duick II, but he certainly shattered a few experts' predictions by sailing to Newport in twenty-seven days. Four years later, when he brought the barely-finished Pen Duick IV (above) to Plymouth, he was voted favourite but never really got started
Photo: Chris Smith

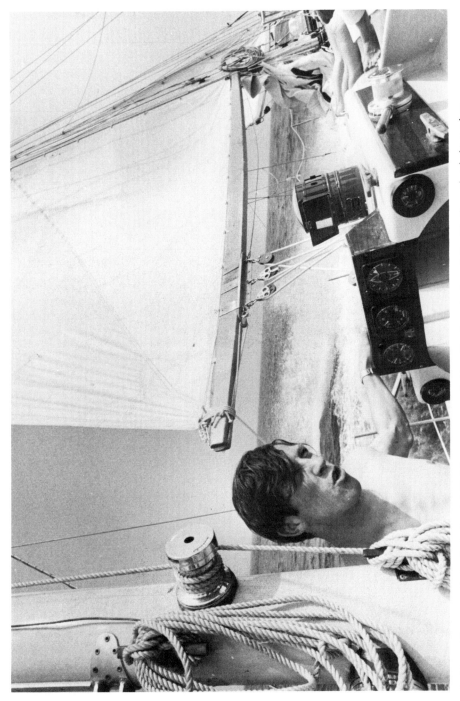

Geoffrey Williams was absolutely single-minded in his determination to win the 1968 Observer Singlehanded at the helm of the 56 foot ketch Sir Thomas Lipton. After the bigger French boats had been forced to retire he underlined the theory that the biggest boat to survive must win the race

Photo: Chris Smith

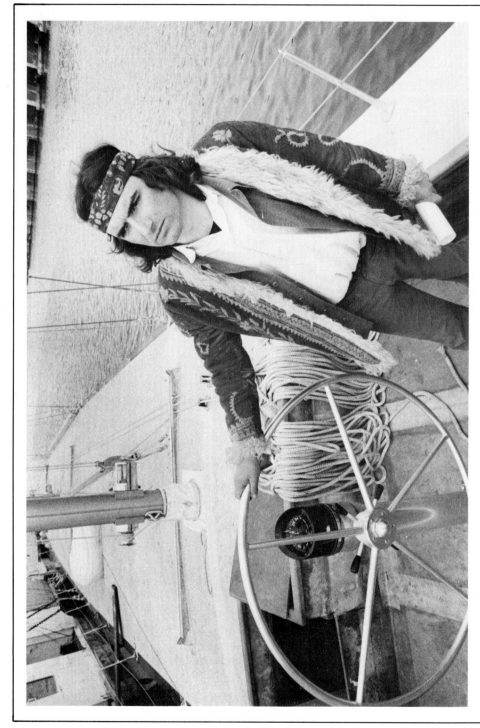

Many people asked whether Jean-Yves Terlain could possibly handle the 128 foot length of Vendredi 13 on his own. But then, they asked the same question when Francis Chichester entered a 39 foot boat for the first Observer race!

Photo: Chris Smith

Marie-Claude Fauroux learned to sail in tiny dinghies – she was a Moth champion. She reckons that strength isn't important in sailing a 35-footer like Aloa VII alone – it's resistance that counts, she says
Photo: Chris Smith

At the start Jean-Yves Terlain kept Vendredi 13 to the windward end of the line and thus well away from the rest of the fleet. But he couldn't shake off the many small powerboats which were intent on getting a close view of the huge schooner

Photo: Chris Smith

Harry Mitchell's yacht Tuloa is no longer in her first youth, but that does not dim the enormous affection the Southsea garage mechanic has for her. Mitchell started the race determined to fulfil a long-felt ambition to sail solo to America, but alas, Tuloa just wasn't up to it

Photo: Chris Smith

Chris Baranowski may not ring many bells here, but in Poland his name is well known, for he works on a Warsaw paper and appears frequently on Polish television. In fact the name for his boat, Polonez, was decided by the children who watch his regular programme

Photo: Henryk Kabit

Mike McMullen remains smiling and ebullient whatever happens. That's no doubt something to do with his rigorous training as a Royal Marines officer in a commando unit. He took sail number 45 because that's the number of his commando group

Photo: Chris Smith

Bruce Webb's schooner Gazelle pushes up a crested quarter wave as she sails hard on the wind during trials
Photo: Chris Smith

Max Barton at the helm of Bristol Fashion.
She may be small but she moves well in a blow
Photo: Neil Libbert

David Blagden in the tiny Willing Griffin.
Despite a hard time on his qualifying cruise,
Blagden was as keen as any to get going from
Plymouth
Photo: Bob Salmon

Bandleader Bob Miller exchanged the spotlights and cheers of the bandstand for the wet, cold, and loneliness of the North Atlantic – and never lost his cheerful disposition and broad smile
Photo: Neil Libbert

Bill Howell changed the name of his catamaran from Golden Cockerel to Tahiti Bill a few weeks before the race, to show that he was no longer sponsored by his 1968 benefactors, the Courage brewery
Photo: Chris Smith

Martin Wills has the bluff solidity about him of a man who has spent many years at sea. The other competitors soon found that he had a good sense of humour too
Photo: Bob Salmon

Brian Cooke was fancied to do well by all the experts. He was sailing a fast boat, the Robert Clark-designed British Steel (which Chay Blyth took nonstop round the world), and because he had performed very well in 1968 by sailing the 32 foot sloop Opus into sixth place in thirty-four days
Photo: Bryn Campbell

supporter of the race and its stout defender against considerable opposition.

It is not really surprising that there was opposition then, or indeed that it continues to this day in some quarters. Consider the implications of organising a singlehanded race. You are encouraging sailors to face alone all the hazards of a passage across the ocean. They may be wrecked in a storm, sunk by collision with an iceberg or passing ship, subjected to the dangers of exposure to wet and cold beyond what they ever imagined, or even starved to death by failing to make port before their limited supplies of food are used up.

At the same time you are encouraging boats onto the high seas which cannot possibly maintain a look-out at all times, which is, strictly speaking, against the letter of the law. And you may well be abetting a situation where rescue services are called upon to risk the lives of their members in an attempt to save one of your singlehanders.

For a sponsoring newspaper there are similar hazards. It is all very well having the title of your publication reproduced from time to time when the race is making good news around the world. But if the news turns sour – a well known sailor is lost at sea or a searching rescue aircraft has to put down disastrously, for example – then you are plumb in the firing line for any criticism.

J R L Anderson is a well known chronicler of the feats of adventurers, particularly of those who sail the oceans or climb mountains. In his excellent book *The Ulysses Factor* he writes, '*The Observer's* sponsorship of the first Singlehanded Transatlantic Race was an act of considerable courage. If anything had gone wrong, if one or more of the competitors had been lost, there would have been a great deal of criticism, questions in Parliament about how to control irresponsible newspapers, an unpleasant fuss. Nothing went wrong and *The Observer's* faith was justified.'

Fortunately, nothing went wrong during the second and third races, either, apart from the sad disappearance of Arthur Piver, the American yacht designer and sailor, when he was carrying out his qualifying cruise for the 1968 race. But obviously this state of affairs cannot continue indefinitely. Sailing alone involves considerable risks and it would be foolish not to face up to them. Sooner or later somebody will be lost competing in the race.

The race organisers are well aware of this fact, and they expect every entrant to face it too. That is why one of the few rules of the race reads 'Yachts must be fully independent and capable of carrying out their own emergency repairs at sea. Crews have no right to expect or demand rescue operations to be launched on their behalf.'

That may sound a harsh ruling, but it could be worse. At the time of the first race Blondie Hasler wanted to make it a condition that competitors had no means of summoning help except visually. 'I realise now that my original idea was too fanatical,' he says. 'But I didn't want any disaster to bring the race into disrepute. And I would still subscribe to that idea both if I were a competitor and in ordinary sailing.'

However, the originator of the Observer Single-handed is by no means so fanatical that he cannot see the other side of the argument about rescue operations for competitors who get into trouble. 'This is a difficult question because I'm sure we all agree that if someone is in distress in the ocean and rescue services are available, then we would want them to do what they could. On the other hand, it seems equally true that if this race were to start involving rescue services every time it was sailed it would be a very good reason for abandoning it altogether.

'The other way of looking at it is to say "The rescue services are raised and paid for the purposes of rescuing people so it does no harm to exercise their skill. This is fine until someone gets killed in the rescue service."'

It is a conflict of motivations that has been debated since the first singlehanded race. And there was a considerable increase in the amount of nervous energy expended at the time of the 1968 race, when several competitors were in distress at sea and three had to be rescued as their boats sank. The detractors were complaining of inexperienced crews and ill-prepared boats; the supporters were pointing out that the RAF and US Air Force planes who searched and found Joan de Kat and Edith Baumann were only too pleased to have dramatic purpose to liven their normally tedious patrol duties. There is no final answer, but it is perhaps salutary to remember that Blondie Hasler once told me he hoped any single-hander who got 'into trouble out of reach of rescue would be content to drown like a gentleman'.

And the vexed question of safety and rescue is not the only one that inspires heated arguments round yacht club bars every four years. What about the old warhorse of commercial sponsorship? Many people think that sponsorship is vital to the health of such an unorthodox event as the Observer Singlehanded. It is argued that it is the only way designers and crews with original ideas about yacht design and gear efficiency can get the money to put their theories into practice, and the race itself is the only major test of such original ideas which is not hedged about with regulations about boat size, handicap ratings, and the rest. How refreshing it is to read that simple sentence in the brief rules issued by the Royal Western: 'Yachts of any size or type may enter, subject to the decision of the organisers', which complements perfectly the printed object of the whole exercise: 'The race is intended to be a sporting event, and to encourage the development of suitable boats, gear, supplies and techniques for singlehanded ocean crossings under sail.'

That is why, says the pro-sponsorship lobby, you must have commercial firms putting up plenty of cash – to allow the bright boys of the design world to fulfil that object. They can then design the unorthodox boats which will make the whole yachting world sit up – like Dick Newick's astonishing proa *Cheers*, which Tom Follett sailed brilliantly into third place in the 1968 race. After all, the winner of the race gets simply a trophy, not a cash reward, so it is unrealistic to expect anyone to build a revolutionary new craft at a cost of many thousands of pounds unless there is some other pay-off. And that pay-off just has to be a publicity kick-back for the sponsoring company that financed the whole operation.

It's a logical argument, but it overlooks one word in the stated object of the race – the word 'sporting'. The race is intended to be a sporting event. The antisponsorship lobby maintains fiercely that no matter how original and interesting its design, the yacht which crosses the Atlantic principally to advertise a drink, a cigarette, or a brand of cosmetics is not really participating in a sporting event. The Royal Western's Race Committee are, of course, very conscious of this dilemma. After the 1968 race they rephrased the rules, saying that they were not averse to the sponsorship of entries and 'are indeed glad of the help that has been given to the competitors in the previous races, which undoubtedly added to the interest in them. Nevertheless they are concerned that this race should remain a sporting event and reserve the right to refuse an entry if it appears that the primary object of it is to promote a commercial project not connected with the object of the race.

'In particular, a yacht owned or sponsored wholly or partly by a group or organisation may not display any emblem or wording that relates specifically to such sponsor other than a house flag.'

That, too, is a logical argument, and enough to deter many a publicity manager who has money in his budget but wants to be sure he is going to get value for it in public recognition. How this ruling worked out in the big build-up to the 1972 race we shall see in a later chapter. It is enough here to recognise that both the sponsoring newspaper and the organising club were concerned to keep the Observer Singlehanded true to the spirit in which it had originally been conceived by Blondie Hasler.

Inherent in that resistance to over-commercialisation lies a serious concern about the pressures that can be put upon a singlehanded sailor who has a heavy commitment to his sponsor. As we have seen, many thousands of pounds can be swallowed up in the building of an experimental boat to go quickly across the Atlantic. Indeed, even the building and equipping of a production yacht for this enterprise is no superficial financial burden.

If a solo sailor does manage to find a commercial sponsor – increasingly difficult these days – does he at the same time sell his independence to take the right decisions at the right time in mid-ocean? It is a question which has had much greater relevance since the tragic story of Donald Crowhurst was revealed.

Crowhurst was 37, a married man with four children. He was an experienced sailor who tried desperately hard in 1968 to raise the financial support which would enable him to sail in the *Sunday Times* race for the Golden Globe, for the first nonstop solo circumnavigation. It was a tremendous struggle, both to raise the money and to get the boat ready to sail by 31 October 1968 – the last possible leaving date. But sail Crowhurst did, at the helm of his 42 foot trimaran *Teignmouth Electron*. The boat was illprepared – there had not been enough time for proper trials and the crew himself admitted 'I have never put to sea in such an unprepared state in my life.'

But it seemed that Donald Crowhurst was even less well prepared for the voyage than his trimaran. He was not satisfied with the boat and certainly far from stable in himself. One of the boatyard workers said later 'He was in a daze. We'd have admired him much more if he'd simply said "I've lost my nerve. Let's drop the whole business." Obviously he was in a blind panic and didn't have the guts to call it off.' That seems now an astute judgement. Crowhurst spent his last night on shore weeping in his wife's arms, but still unable to take the awful decision to call off the enterprise which involved so many other people relying upon him.

The result is history. Crowhurst's trimaran was found deserted in mid-Atlantic in July 1969 with logs that indicated that he had falsified his reports to London, having never left the Atlantic, and then become quite unstable in mind as the significance of his actions became fully clear to him. He probably ended his life by stepping off the stern of *Teignmouth Electron*.

In *The Ulysses Factor* J R L Anderson writes, 'One may feel now that someone should have stopped Crowhurst, but it is hard to say who, or how. And if Crowhurst had insisted on sailing, by what authority could he have been held? None. One may feel this or that unhappy adventurer should have been stopped, but ... is there any moral basis for interfering with a man's right to risk his life, if he chooses, for a dream?'

Perhaps not, but is it not also true that intensive commercialisation could well interfere with a man's right to *save* his life if he chooses? Blondie Hasler is pertinent on this topic. 'As I don't like being sponsored anyhow – even if I could get sponsorship – I am bound to be sailing in small uncompetitive boats until I win a football pool. I have a considerable aversion to being sponsored for the obvious reasons – the Crowhurst reasons. For me it would be horrible to start a transatlantic race and feel that you had to do well in order to give your sponsors a return for their money. The greatest freedom I value is the freedom to give up off the Eddystone light if you don't like it.'

Fortunately, it is a freedom that a large proportion of the competitors in the Observer Singlehanded share, for more than half of them sail in their own uncompetitive boats just for the sake of having gone solo to America rather than in the hope of winning the main trophy. Blondie Hasler again: 'Yes, they have always been the majority. The majority of this year's starters are people who have no reasonable hope of winning. But they have got a good hope of winning the handicap award. I think this is fine.'

Opinions will always vary about the value of sponsorship and the pressures it puts upon the singlehander. But then, commercial pressures bear as much, if not more, on other types of sportsmen who need money to be able to compete. The racing driver is the obvious example, but it applies to virtually every class of professional sportsman and to many who are nominally amateurs as well.

Yet surely the singlehanded race to America is something rather different from any other sporting activity. No matter what the increase in long-distance solo sailing, there are still few enough people who have actually crossed the Atlantic under sail alone for it to be a considerable achievement in its own right. It is still enough to compete rather than to win, and for this reason it is right that the Royal Western Yacht Club, and *The Observer*, should stress that all-important word 'sporting' and turn a wary eye on entries for the race which seem to be motivated purely by a commercial purpose.

4 The First Race – 1960

Commercial sponsorship played very little part in the first Observer Singlehanded. Though the word had got around the yachting world that it was definitely to take place, the public's interest was scarcely touched until just before the start. Nevertheless, as it did become known that a race would definitely take place from Plymouth, beginning on Saturday 11 June 1960, the enquiries started to come in from many countries. Strongest interest was in Britain, of course, but there were also letters from the United States, France, Germany, Denmark, and Canada. The list soon mounted to over 50 requests for information, but when the starting date drew near there were just eight entries. Of those only five actually set sail for New York.

The finish that year was off the Ambrose lightship at the southernmost tip of Long Island, and as the little band of solo sailors made their final preparations in Plymouth's Millbay Dock, there were many discussions about the best route to take. There were just four sailors there then, for the Frenchman Jean Lacombe did not arrive in Plymouth until the evening before the start and actually set out on the 16th.

Favourite to win was Francis Chichester and his *Gipsy Moth III* – an ocean racing yawl 39 feet in length – what seemed then about the biggest boat one man could handle. The other three yachts already in Plymouth measured 25 feet. Blondie Hasler's modified Folkboat was called *Jester* because, he said, she was 'such a bloody joke'. She had an unstayed mast and single Chinese lugsail of 240 square feet area.

Val Howells' yacht was also a Folkboat, though conventionally sloop rigged, and the third of the 25-footers was *Cardinal Vertue*, a Vertue class sloop belonging to Dr David Lewis. Lewis was born in England but went to New Zealand when only two years old, so he considers himself a Kiwi. He is short, dark, and obviously tough. He at least knew that his boat was capable of doing the Atlantic crossing, because Humphrey Barton had sailed his *Vertue XXXV* to New York from Falmouth with Kevin O'Riordan ten years earlier.

Jean Lacombe's yacht was a 21 foot centreboard sloop. It had been ordered by an owner in New York. 'I am just driving it across for him,' said Lacombe, who had crossed the Atlantic solo before – in 1956 from Toulon to New York.

Lacombe is not a big man either. In fact, the only one of the five starters who fitted the conventional picture of the dashing, muscular seaman was the Welshman Val Howells, who is tall and hugely bearded – 'the black-bearded Viking' was Chichester's favourite name for him.

Well might they spend hours talking about which route to take, for the North Atlantic is a mass of contradictions for the sailor travelling east–west. The conventional route to New York in the old days of square-riggers was down the European coast to the Canaries, across to the West Indies then up the eastern seaboard to the capital. By that route you can expect reaching winds most of the way. But it is about 5,000 miles sailing, as opposed to the great circle route which is a little under 3,000 miles. (It has to be not quite a great circle because a direct great circle route crosses Newfoundland.)

The problem with this northern route is that it is into the teeth of the prevailing south-westerlies and also involves the persistently foggy areas of the Grand Banks off Newfoundland, as well as some danger of meeting the icebergs which float down the Davis Strait from Greenland and Baffin Island during June and July. Once through those hazards, though, there is in theory a Labrador Current which helps the boats home down the east coast of the North American continent, though few competitors ever seem to get much benefit from it.

A compromise solution between the great circle (or nothern) route and the far south trade wind route is to sail southwest to the Azores and then across to America. It is certainly warmer and sometimes avoids those persistent headwinds, but it is longer (about 3,600 miles to New York) and involves crossing the west–east flowing Gulf Stream not far from the finish.

Most competitors feel that the shortest distance is the most attractive and keep near to the great circle route, but it is significant that Tom Follett and *Cheers* came third in the 1968 race by taking the Azores route. What's more, because Follett had to alter course less frequently than those passing further north, he actually sailed fewer miles to get to Newport. For all that, the 1960, '64, and '68 races were all won by yachts taking the northern route.

So it is not surprising to discover that the experienced quartet that talked freely about their intentions to each other in Plymouth back in 1960 were all intending to go by way of the great circle. That is to say, three of them were talking freely. Chichester was being what David Lewis calls 'cagey'. But he gave the game away by going shopping with Val Howells and buying a length of fishing net to drape round the stanchions of *Gipsy Moth III* to catch, he said, the flying fish that would skim aboard. Of course, flying fish are only found far to the south, so the rest all knew then that the wily 58-year-old Chichester was intending to go north!

Blondie Hasler's plan was to go further north than any of the others, perhaps as high as the 55th parallel, in the hope of being on the northern edge of the Atlantic depressions and thus possibly pick up some easterlies. The other three were basing their decision to take the great circle on the American pilot charts. But Hasler said, depressingly, 'I don't believe the winds have ever read the American pilot charts.'

At 10 a.m. on the morning of Saturday 11 June 1960, the first Observer Singlehanded race began. Experienced ocean racer that he is, Blondie Hasler had *Jester* perfectly positioned on the line and crossed it first, followed by Lewis in *Cardinal Vertue* and Howells in *Eira*. But the extra length of *Gipsy Moth III* was not to be denied for long. She quickly surged through the others and headed away towards the Lizard.

Lewis did not get so far that first day. Just 3½ hours after the start and not far past the Eddystone light his mast snapped cleanly 12 feet above the deck, the upper 22 feet crashing into the sea over the port quarter. Dismayed but not defeated, he hoisted a jury rig and made back for Plymouth, where Mashford's yard promised to get him going by the Monday again – and did. So even with that delay David Lewis was still ahead of Jean Lacombe, who stayed in Plymouth until Thursday.

When he did go, Lacombe said he was taking the Azores route, though by the end of the first week he had not progressed much and was still in the Channel north of Jersey.

Meanwhile Chichester had made the best progress, keeping well to his great circle route despite being forced southwest in the first few days. Lewis was on the same course but, obviously, a long way behind. Hasler had gone round the Fastnet and was heading northwest while Howells had also been pushed to the southwest and seemed to be heading for a route not far north of the Azores line.

Howells had had his problems too. The lashings on his battery in the forecastle had shrunk and torn the battery apart, spilling acid over his clothes and food and depriving him of navigation lights and radio. Back at home, there was little for Chris Brasher to report in *The Observer*, even two weeks after the start, except that the finishing line had disappeared! An American freighter had rammed the Ambrose light vessel and sent it to the bottom with beacon flashing and sirens blaring.

But plenty had been going on at sea, even if the news was not getting through. Francis Chichester later wrote of force 8 and 9 winds the second night out, which he reported in his log with customary relish: 'My word, some whacking big seas hit the hull at times. The noise these seas make is terrific. So much that I several times started getting out of my berth thinking the yacht had been struck by a steamer or that the mast had gone overboard.' In the first week he was disappointed with his progress and after 12 days reported 'We have only been making four knots with the number three jib and the main reefed. Nor are we going in the right direction. The wind is straight from New York. Yesterday's run was the worst yet – 71 miles. Goodbye to my hopes of a fast passage.'

But his progress was still good enough to put him ahead of the field – and right in the path of a storm. It arrived at *Gipsy Moth III* on 25 June. 'The din was appalling,' he wrote in his diary. 'A high-pitched screech dominating everything, spray peppering everywhere and seas hitting periodically with the bonk of a big drum.'

He spent more than five hours stripping the sails from *Gipsy Moth*, then shackled a motor tyre to the anchor chain and paid it out over the stern. 'I concluded it was not the slightest use. The anchor chain left a white wake as it cut through the water. Three knots, I thought. I put the wind now at 100 m.p.h. . . . I hope those other poor devils have not been caught in this. I am sure it would be much worse in a smaller boat. Personally, I am flogged to the bone.'

The smaller boats were having their share of the bad weather, too. On 27 June, when Chichester was through the worst and able to get on with repairing his self-steering gear, his position was 48½°N, 34°W, getting on for half way across the ocean. Lewis was at 50°N, 25°W, about 375 miles behind, having come through his first gale – the eastern margin of the low pressure system that had given *Gipsy Moth III* such a hard time.

Hasler was by this time well north at 56°N, 37°W, 450 miles away to the northwest. His laconic description of this part of the voyage is a nice contrast to Chichester's. 'In a very boring gale that has been blowing for three days and shows no sign of stopping. If I were cruising I should be comfortably hoveto. As things are, I am driving the poor little thing into a filthy breaking sea with four reefs down.'

On the same day Howells was nearing the Azores, having completed his first 1,000 miles (but on the longer route). 'My mind is boggling at the thought of spending another five weeks in this manner,' he wrote. 'Have finished all the reading matter – very, very bored.'

Jean Lacombe, at the same time, was just 11 days out of Plymouth and had reached the latitude of Cape Finisterre on his way towards the Azores. So 16 days after the start the five singlehanders had scattered across the ocean like dandelion seeds on the wind.

By the end of the third week Brasher was reporting odd sightings that put the picture into some perspective for those waiting anxiously at home. It was obvious that *Gipsy Moth III* was leading the field, about 160 miles ahead of *Jester*, away to the north. But the little Folkboat had made good progress, covering 1,500 miles or more.

Far away south, Howells was making better speed after a slow getaway, with a spell of 100 miles and more each day. Lewis was struggling through a belt of calms and Jean Lacombe's little *Cap Horn* was following roughly in Howells wake, about 300 miles behind. It began to look like a struggle between Chichester and Hasler, though at that stage it was difficult to say how much Hasler's loop to the north had helped or hindered.

Certainly Hasler's rig had enabled him to avoid the worst effects of going so far away from the great circle. It gets very cold up at 56 degrees North, even in July, so being able to control that single lugsail so easily standing waist-high out of the central hatch, rather than scrambling about on deck manhandling canvas, must have made a big difference.

And this is what Blondie Hasler feels the single-handed race is all about. Before the 1972 race I asked him if he were disappointed with the way boats had developed throughout the four races. 'Not disappointed at all,' he replied. 'But the development has pushed ahead very strongly with making boats longer and lighter, which is fine, while not very much has been done to make boats easier or more comfortable to sail. Two of my interests are what you could call an automatic rig – a rig which can be reefed, furled, unreefed, and set again without clawing at canvas (the few other Chinese sail boats which have been entered for the race are the only ones which have tried to achieve this – all others have involved somebody on deck clawing at the sails) – and secondly enclosure. To me it is efficient as well as pleasant for the watchkeeping position to be enclosed, and I am totally committed to this idea that you look out of a circular hatch and have your head protected by a pram cover on a circular ring which you rotate to windward. That combines efficiency with comfort – you have your eyes and ears out in the open air so you can use your senses.

'A few people in this race have used Perspex domes for protection, but most still struggle into their oilskins, go on deck, come back and struggle out of them again. I thought that everyone would think as I did – that one would like to sail with the minimum of exertion and the minimum of fatigue, but this has not proved true.

'Many of the competitors actually seem to revel in the fact that they are engaged in a test of endurance and strength. Fair enough – it is a sport, and it is perfectly reasonable for it to be exhausting – as most sports are. But as a test of stamina doesn't happen to be the way I see a test of sailing – I regard it as unseamanlike to get exhausted, or to get cold and wet.'

In that first race, Hasler certainly practised what he has always preached. He pushed away up to the north, hunting his easterlies, but he was never in danger of letting the elements get him down. His log remained taciturnly cheerful.

'I had always intended to sail a high northern route, but now I've allowed myself to get pushed even further north, rather than make an unprofitable tack to the southward. Nearest land Greenland 280 miles away, and it feels like it. I get out my banjo-ukelele and improvise a song entitled "Meet me tonight in Greenland".'

As the first week of July went by Chichester and Hasler entered the area of the North Atlantic where the charts carry a red line marked 'Extreme limit of drifting ice, July'. The skipper of *Gipsy Moth III* contacted Cape Race to report his position 50 miles S S W of the Cape which is the southeast tip of Newfoundland. He had completed 2,100 miles and was averaging 78 miles a day, with about 800 miles to go. Hasler was then making his way south towards Cape Race, best part of a week's sailing behind Chichester. Lewis was on the fringe of the ice area just below 50 degrees North, and the other two were west of the Azores, Howells further south than Lacombe.

At the end of the fifth week Brasher was estimating that either Chichester or Hasler could reach New York by the 18th or 19th of July, but that was wishful thinking. In fact, the last beat into New York took a lot more time than most people expected. Chichester recorded gloomily in his diary: 'Those who took the Azores route will all be in New York by now. I sighted my first land today since the Eddystone. It was Block Island at the entrance to Long Island Sound . . . I quite understand why people used to, and still do, go into retreat. During a month alone I think at last you become a real person and you are concerned with the real values of life.' Next day, 21 July, he contacted the Coast Guard and said he expected to cross the finishing line about 1330.

'Twenty-four miles to go,' he wrote. 'What do you think? Will that black-bearded Viking be in already?' In fact the Welsh Viking was not making anything like such good progress. First, his boat had a persistent leak, which necessitated continual pumping. Then when he was northeast of Bermuda and sailing well reefed through a belt of squalls, he suddenly found *Eira* laid flat by an unexpected gust – mast and sails pressed into the sea. When at last Howells righted the boat he found that his chronometer was gone, so he had no means of discovering his longitude. He decided to run his latitude down to

Bermuda and arrived there 30 July, leaving again on 5 August.

So Howells actually finished fourth, behind Hasler and Lewis. Hasler arrived in New York on 30 July, 48 days out from Plymouth. His diary is the best evidence of the soundness of his theories. 'I am homing towards the Ambrose light vessel entirely by the sound of her diaphone fog signal, one blast every 15 seconds . . . I feel absolutely fresh, and only faintly unwilling to plunge back into civilisation. My experimental boat has done better than I would ever have dared to hope, and my head is full of wonderful bits of design for my next boat – for *Jester* is only a beginning. I've never had to go on deck in an emergency, or in bad weather. The wind vane steering gear has become a part of me, something I shall never again sail without.'

Brasher was in America to report the finish and noted how happy and fit Hasler seemed – in sharp contrast to Chichester who, he said, had worked incredibly hard and arrived in New York with a deep sense of weariness about him.

While the leaders were closing New York, the others were still having their adventures. Lacombe was suffering a severe gale followed by calms, so he sailed north to avoid the August hurricanes. Lewis had a brush, literally, with a Canadian frigate which stopped to hail him cheerily and also blanketed out all his wind. He could not avoid colliding with the steel hull and had his lower port spreader torn out of its socket in the process.

When he got under way again, he was forced inside Sable Island and along the Nova Scotian coast in thick fog. He then decided to sail through Pollock Rip at night, in fog and with a vicious tide under his keel. But even though he went aground once he managed to get out of trouble and sail down the coast inside Martha's Vineyard and so into New York to finish third in 56 days. Two chapters in David Lewis's book *The Ship Would Not Travel Due West* carry headings that indicate the hazards of his voyage – 'Thundering Surf' and 'Unfriendly Coast'. The course he took then was not allowed in this year's race, for the Observer Singlehanded competitors must now leave the Nantucket light to starboard.

Howells finished the course on 13 August and Lacombe arrived on the 24th, having been taken in tow by the Coast Guard for some distance because of a threat of high seas and a hurricane. So all five boats made the passage and the sceptics were eating their words – not only about the lack of disaster but also about the speed of the first boat home. Chichester's 40 days seemed astounding, even though he said at his press conference that he had been aiming at 30 days. 'I hoped to set a time that would be difficult to beat,' he said. 'Every time I tried to point *Gipsy Moth* to New York the wind blew dead on her nose. It was like trying to reach a doorway with a man in it aiming a hose at you. It was much tougher than I thought.'

In the perspective of later races, those 1960 times are not so impressive. Chichester crossed to New York again two years later and took a week off his previous time. In 1968 Brian Cooke sailed the 32 foot sloop *Opus* to Newport in just over 34 days, while there was general concern for the life of Michael Ritchey and *Jester* when he took more than 50 days to finish the course – eight years earlier Lewis was considered to have done extremely well to get to New York in 54 days actual sailing time. And there were two more finishers after him!

The lesson of that first race is simple – Hasler stated at the end that he had been at the tiller of *Jester* for just one hour during the whole passage. His self-steering gear did the rest. All the competitors used self-steering equipment, of course, though Hasler admitted later that his could have sailed him to disaster when he believed the evidence of one sun sight rather than his dead reckoning. He described it as 'a lousy bit of navigation near Ireland'. After taking his sight he came to the conclusion he was well clear of the Fastnet and lay down, even though he could hear the fog gun booming through the mist. Suddenly *Jester* put herself about. Hasler looked out and there was the rocky coast 400 yards away on the fringe of the visibility.

Humphrey Barton quotes a pertinent piece of doggerel in his book *Atlantic Adventurers*:

Poor old Bill lies deep in the sea
He went fast asleep as Rose sailed free.
The self-steering gear held her true on course
T'was the steamer she hit brought news of her loss!

	Final placing in 1960 Observer Singlehanded			
Place	Yacht	Crew	Arrival	Days taken
1	*Gipsy Moth III*	Francis Chichester	21/7	40
2	*Jester*	Blondie Hasler	30/7	48
3	*Cardinal Vertue*	David Lewis	6/8	56
4	*Eira*	Val Howells	13/8	63
5	*Cap Horn*	Jean Lacombe	24/8	74

Cardinal Vertue put back to Plymouth with a damaged mast and set sail again on 13 June. *Eira* put into Bermuda for new chronometer and battery 29 July–5 August. *Cap Horn* left Plymouth 16 June; was later taken in tow for a few hours off the American coast because of high seas and winds.

5 The 1964 Race

The second Observer Singlehanded race was as different from the first as a cup final is from a fourth division relegation scrabble. That is not to imply any lack of quality in the first race or its contestants – it is a difference of public awareness.

In 1960 there were four Britons and one Frenchman disputing a very parochial sort of competition. *The Observer* was the only newspaper to give the race any coverage and after the mild excitement of the start interest at home quickly waned. It is difficult now to remember that Francis Chichester was known only to those who had a keen interest in flying, navigation, or sailing and the other contestants were simply names – except possibly to those who remembered Blondie Hasler's wartime exploits.

But by 1964 many things had changed. Francis Chichester and David Lewis had published books about the first race (Val Howells' required a longer gestation) and Chichester had crossed alone to America in 1962 in 33 days. These events had caught the public imagination and there was suddenly a much greater awareness of the endeavour required in sailing solo to America.

The newspapers recognised it too. The *Guardian*, urged on by J R L Anderson, signed up Chichester and David Lewis to radio daily reports, and the *Daily Mail* made a contract with Mike Ellison. The *Daily Express* stood by for news reports from Val Howells, while *The Observer*, naturally, was devoting a lot of space to the child it had nurtured.

The race now had a different standing in yachting circles too. As the entries came in it was quickly apparent that the Singlehanded had become an international affair. Arthur Piver, the American designer of multihull boats who narrowly missed starting in 1960, was determined to go this time; Bill Howell, an Australian dentist living in London, put in his entry; Axel Pederson, the 45-year-old Dane who had already sailed round the world, had written to say he was a starter. (As it turned out, Piver again missed the race. He was held up in Bermuda.)

Perhaps most significant of all, there were now two French entrants: Jean Lacombe again, with a 21 foot sloop called *Golif*, and Lieutenant Eric Tabarly of the French Navy, with a 44 foot ketch called *Pen Duick II*. The important point about Tabarly's entry was that for the first time a boat had been built specially for the race.

Pen Duick II was made of marine ply to provide a light boat that could combine a comparatively long waterline length (about 32 feet) with a small amount of canvas, for ease of handling. She was also ketch rigged so that a solo sailor could handle sail changes easily. Weighing only 6½ tons, she had a sail plan which gave her 620 square feet of canvas – modest enough, but sufficient to propel that long and light hull impressively quickly. The sail plan included both foresail and jib, to help keep the boat moving well during sail changes and to provide a greater variety of sail combinations for best use of the prevailing conditions.

Tabarly also included some innovations on the boat for ease of handling – cleats for securing foresail halliards, for example, and a special roller gear for his spinnaker halliard. For the crew there was a narrow cockpit and a small cabin with low roof. There was also a Perspex dome in that roof through which Tabarly could look out when at the helm – a wheel similar to a car steering wheel.

It all looked impressively thorough to the other competitors, especially when they learned of the concentrated study the Frenchman had made of routes and weather conditions, and found out how intensively he had trained for the race.

Tabarly himself was as impressive as his boat. Stocky (5 feet 4 inches) and solid, his tight-cropped curly hair seemed to bristle with determination. The 32-year-old exuded that Breton toughness that makes a man formidable irrespective of his size. *Pen Duick*, by the way, is Breton for 'little black head', the popular local name for a tomtit in Brittany. But *Pen Duick* was far from little. She was the biggest boat in the fleet – and there could be no doubt that her skipper intended to win.

For all that, Francis Chichester started favourite again. He was still in *Gipsy Moth III*, even though his plans were already afoot for the *Gipsy Moth IV* that would take him round the world a couple of years later. But the mark III had been re-rigged by John Illingworth, and was faster than ever.

In fact, all the 1960 competitors were going again; Hasler in *Jester*, while the other three had different boats. Val Howells had borrowed a new 35 foot sloop called *Akka* – and sold his steak and lobster restaurant to cover expenses. She was steel-built in the Van der Stadt yard and Howells put it about that she was more comfortable than fast. But Tabarly for one was not taken in. 'I know quite a few Dutch boats of that kind which are comfortable and still fast,' he said later. He was proved right.

Jean Lacombe's *Golif* had a glassfibre hull, and as in 1960 his was the smallest boat in the race. David Lewis had changed his allegiance from monohulls to multihulls, entering a catamaran called *Rehu Moana* (Maori for sea spray). The 40 foot boat had been specially designed for Lewis by Colin Mudie and built the year before. She was actually intended for a three-year circumnavigation that Lewis planned to make with his family after the '64 race, so she was stoutly built. Indeed she was really too heavy to offer much competition to the fast single-hulled boats like *Gipsy Moth III*, *Pen Duick II*, and *Akka*.

But there was another threat from a multihull. Derek Kelsall, then a 31-year-old oil engineer, had entered a new trimaran ketch, 35 feet long and 20 feet in the beam, to Arthur Piver's design. Piver reported that his own trimaran *Bird* had reached a speed of 30 knots in the Atlantic under the most favourable conditions – a sobering thought for the monohullers.

And there was a third multihull for the '64 race – another catamaran. It was sailed by Michael Butterfield, a 32-year-old lawyer from Cobham who became the mystery man of the race, shunning publicity and wanting to race anonymously if possible. In the event, he simply attracted more attention. The paradox of legal ethics. His boat, *Misty Miller*, had gone very well in the 1963 Fastnet Race and she looked a real menace to the monohulls if the winds favoured her.

So the mono versus multihull controversy had really moved into the Observer Singlehanded field. Blondie Hasler was delighted. He wrote in *The Observer* that he thought this race would provide some very interesting comparisons. 'Derek Kelsall

in his 35 foot trimaran will have a chance of silencing those wicked critics who whisper that such craft have so far only crossed oceans by blowing downwind at modest speeds and are not good at serious windward work in rough weather,' he said.

Hasler also remarked that the average size of boat was much bigger for the second race. Of the 15 starters, three were more than 40 feet overall, with *Pen Duick II* biggest of all at 44 feet; most (nine yachts) were between 30 and 40 feet long, and only four were under 30 feet. There should have been an even bigger starter than Tabarly's – a 48 foot gaff ketch which had been entered by an American radio engineer called C R McLendon, but unfortunately there was an explosion aboard this somewhat antiquated vessel when she was lying at Yarmouth three weeks before the start, so she was not fit to sail.

The founder of the race took the opportunity to restate his theories about the need for a simple rig and protection for the helmsman. 'Yachtsmen cling doggedly to the belief that you cannot sail a boat properly unless the spray is running down inside your vest. This is the reverse of the truth,' he wrote. Hasler also admitted there was one enemy that the solo sailor would probably never conquer – the motion of a small boat in heavy weather. 'It can reduce living on board to a question of survival rather than comfort. What seems to be needed now is a sort of dentist's chair below decks in which you can cook, eat, navigate, read and even sleep with your whole body supported against the motion and all your muscles relaxed. But this might interfere with what is undoubtedly the world's most efficient slimming treatment.'

Hasler's dentist's chair is, of course, a more sophisticated version of the traditional sailor's hammock. It is interesting to note that not long after these words were written Francis Chichester had not only his stove but also a table and chair mounted on gimbals aboard *Gipsy Moth IV*, so that he could cook, eat, and write at a natural angle when the boat was heeled as much as 35 degrees.

Of the other singlehanders who moved out to the start line on the morning of Saturday 23 May 1964, the details were sparse but intriguing. There was a 55-year-old fruit merchant from Southsea by the name of Alec Rose, for example, in his 36 foot cutter *Lively Lady*. Rose had learned respect for the sea on wartime North Atlantic convoys. Then there was the Australian Bill Howell and his 30 foot yacht *Stardrift*. At 38, Howell was already one of the most experienced singlehanders in the world, having taken his *Wanderer II* across the Atlantic and up to Vancouver by way of the Panama Canal and Tahiti. Many people knew him as Tahiti Bill. *Stardrift* was a conventional cutter, built in 1937 and displacing 8 tons.

Mike Ellison originally intended to sail his own boat *Blue Haze* in the 1964 race. But he was offered the use of *Ilala* and thought she had a better chance. Blondie Hasler certainly approved, for *Ilala* was a 36 foot, glassfibre hulled, two-masted schooner fitted with Chinese lugsails. Bob Bunker's *Vanda Caelea* was another of those Volkswagens of the sea, the Folkboat. Bunker, then 28, worked at the London Guinness brewery and aimed to get across in 50 days because he had only 48 days' supply of Guinness. The firm offered four dozen bottles to each of the other competitors so that they would not be at a disadvantage!

Yet another cutter was sailed by Geoffrey Chaffey. *Ericht 2* was built in 1938 – just seven years younger than her crew – and measured 31 feet. Chaffey was born in Calcutta and at the time of the race was curator of the Birla Planetarium there. Axel Pederson's *Marco Polo* was a 28 foot ketch which actually sailed into Plymouth Sound as the other 14 competitors were leaving on the race – the voyage from Denmark to Plymouth took longer than he had planned.

Finally there was *Tammie Norie*, the 41 foot ketch to be sailed by Dr Robin McCurdy. He had won the Cruising Association Knight Cup for his singlehanded cruise to the Faroes the year before and looked a formidable challenge. But it was not to be.

If anyone remained unconvinced that the Observer Singlehanded had become a major yachting event, that grey Saturday May morning would surely have converted them. The Sound was thronged with boats milling about near the start line – sailing and power boats, ocean racers, Naval barges, launches and dinghies, all packed with spectators. The Hoe and beaches were dense with more onlookers, while overhead helicopters and light aircraft buzzed noisily round so that the photographers could pick out the wheat of the competitors from the cheering chaff.

A light easterly wind helped the singlehanders over the line – ideal conditions for the multihulls.

In fact, Kelsall's *Folatre* made the best start, with Hasler and Chichester close behind. Tabarly was not far away and soon had a huge spinnaker billowing in the light breeze. It was enough to take him past *Gipsy Moth* and *Jester* and start gaining on Kelsall's *Folatre*. The shape of things to come.

The fourteen yachts (with Pederson's *Marco Polo* to follow) were headed for Newport. After the 1960 race it was thought sensible to move the finish north to avoid the crowded shipping lanes near New York. At the same time one course mark was added to the sailing instructions: 'thence to Newport, passing south of Nantucket'. This was to avoid the possibility of any competitor getting involved in the hazardous navigation north of Nantucket Island and Martha's Vineyard which had nearly proved disastrous to David Lewis four years earlier.

But the first disaster came even more quickly than in the 1960 race. Howells' *Akka* was rammed by a spectator craft and he had to turn back for repairs to his boom and self-steering gear – a loss of five hours. It was not the end of his bad luck. Four days later a block broke at the top of his mainmast. He climbed up to repair it but there was such a heavy swell that he had to give up the attempt. He then sailed to Baltimore, County Cork, and set out from there once more on 29 May after repairs.

That Howells eventually finished third after such a disappointing start is a tribute both to his determination and his fine seamanship. He also showed in the next few weeks that he had made a very accurate assessment of his rivals in Millbay Dock before the start. The picture that emerged in British press reports was clouded by the fact that certain singlehanders were reporting by radio daily while others sailed on in silence.

This meant that Tabarly's position was never very clear, but Chichester, Lewis, Howells, and Ellison were in constant touch. Inevitably, it seemed that the race was between them. The journalists were hesitant to hedge their bets with conditional clauses about Tabarly, even though he was known to have moved ahead of Chichester at the start and was later sighted in mid-ocean 160 miles ahead of *Gipsy Moth III*'s position.

But Howells was not fooled. On 14 June, five days before Tabarly actually sailed victoriously into Newport, Doddy Hay of *The Observer* was writing that Chichester was set to repeat his 1960 victory.

Yet he also reported a conversation with Howells in which the Welshman said, characteristically, 'Tabarly boyo; that's the fellow I'd put my wild money on. I make him a day ahead of Francis, and what's more I think Francis knows it. Tabarly has a magnificent boat, he's a fine sailor and he's superbly fit. And don't forget Blondie Hasler and the Australian, Howell – both these boys ought to be somewhere up front. I'm sure one of these three will win, probably Tabarly. He'll beat Chichester, break the record and be tying up in America around the 21st June.' He was just two days adrift.

But to be fair, Chichester had recognised the danger from Tabarly also. Just five days after the start he reported to the *Guardian*: 'Tabarly is the dark horse in this race and I think I can hear him galloping through the night. If my senses tell me right I can make him out 120 miles to the north.' His senses were not far out.

By that time – 28 May – the pattern of the race had already been established. Tabarly had taken the lead, sailing just north of the great circle route. Chichester was making good progress not far behind – he reported 133 miles made good in the previous 24 hours – while Lewis was about 65 miles behind *Gipsy Moth III* and Ellison another 35 behind *Rehu Moana*. Howells was in trouble and making for Baltimore – the pressmen were prematurely writing him off. Pederson had started, three days late.

It was a fateful day for Kelsall. He had covered 550 miles from Plymouth and could just have been leading Tabarly when *Folatre* hit something under water and broke a rudder. It might have been a log, or possibly a whale. 'I hope there is a whale with a sore head somewhere out there,' he said when he arrived back in Plymouth on 4 June. He reported some impressive day runs with the trimaran – one of 165 miles. Several times he had been bowling along well at 15 knots.

Unfortunately Kelsall was not able to set out again for Newport until 19 June – the day Tabarly arrived – but he then made an impressively fast crossing of 35 days. If he could have done that first time he would have finished fourth.

As Kelsall was limping back to Plymouth and May turned to June, the leaders were romping across the ocean. Tabarly was sighted 1,080 miles from Plymouth after nine days, and Chichester was reckoned to be less than 100 miles behind him. Howells was reported setting out from Ireland along the Hasler line – the far northern route – in an effort to catch the pack. It was a wise move, for *Jester* was already going well up there, helped by day after day of easterlies, and soon Howells was reporting runs of 150 and more miles a day. By the end of the week (7 June) he calculated that he had made up 300 miles on Chichester's position. But he still thought Tabarly was ahead.

Chichester was slowed by a leak in the hull for about half a day and then pushed on well, making light work of the short storm that hit most of the leaders on 5 June.

There was another heavy blow on the 8th which reduced *Gipsy Moth III* to bare poles but caused jubilation aboard *Rehu Moana*. Lewis reported that the catamaran had handled splendidly in the bad weather – 'a tremendous sea boat'. But it was still a patchy picture. The Frenchman's exact whereabouts were a mystery; little was known of Bill Howell and *Stardrift*; nothing was known of Alec Rose's *Lively Lady*, while mere smatterings of news drifted through about the backmarkers. Robin McCurdy returned to Plymouth on 11 June with broken-down electrical equipment and chronometer – essential navigation aids. He set out again but retired at the Scillies, realising that he hadn't a hope of catching the others.

Chaffey's *Ericht 2* broke a stay on her mainmast and he put into the Azores for repairs, as did Butterfield and *Misty Miller*. Bunker's *Vanda Caelea* was making slow progress on the Azores route and Pederson was behind him. Lacombe plugged on bravely on the great circle route, but obviously his 21 foot craft could not match the daily mileages of the leaders.

The picture came into sharp focus for those at home on the morning of 16 June. The papers which dropped on the mat that day carried news of Tabarly at last. He had been sighted by the Royal Canadian Air Force just 350 miles from Newport and 160 miles ahead of Chichester. If he could maintain his average of 100 miles a day he would be first over the finishing line at Newport on the 19th. He could, and did.

It was a fine, fast crossing in just over 27 days. So fast, indeed, that *Pen Duick II* sailed into a harbour crammed with 143 yachts of the Bermuda Race fleet about to set off on the final race of that year's Onion

Patch series. Nobody had thought one of the single-handers could arrive in Newport so quickly. Francis Chichester, having sent a congratulatory radio message to Tabarly, followed him home in three minutes under 30 days – just making his personal target – and three days later Val Howells sailed in through the rain. The belt of easterlies he found on the high northern route had enabled the Welshman to make up all the time lost at the start and in Ireland. So much for a boat that was more comfortable than fast!

Fourth to finish was the quiet but determined Alec Rose, who had managed not only to keep his *Lively Lady* going remarkably well for 36 days but also to keep out of sight of the spotting aircraft for the previous fortnight. Then a 14-hour spell saw three more boats in: Hasler's *Jester*, Howell's *Stardrift*, and Lewis's *Rehu Moana*. *Jester* had gone at a spanking pace for the first 2,000 miles but then had a dreary time beating to windward through the fog and ice of the Grand Banks and eastern seaboard.

Tabarly became an instant hero. As well as the Legion of Honour award from President de Gaulle, he received thousands of more homely tributes from the world's press and the people of Newport. He did not know he was in the lead in the race until the press boats found him the morning he finished. He had tried to use his radio transmitter only once – when his self-steering gear broke eight days out from Plymouth. 'I do not like these radio instruments,' he said with a Gallic shrug. The full impact of what he said sank in only slowly – Tabarly had actually made this phenomenally fast crossing without self-steering after the first 1,000 miles. He had not slept for more than 90 minutes at a time during the whole voyage and for the 48 hours before crossing the finishing line he had not slept at all.

The tributes from his fellow-competitors were generous, too. Howells said 'That is just how it should be. It is only by following the French approach to this race that we'll ever gain more from it than fun for the participants. If gear and method and design are to be improved so that all yachtsmen benefit from our experience, we must treat it as seriously as Tabarly has done.' Francis Chichester's comment was rather more idiomatic: 'He's a cracking good

Place	Yacht	Crew	Arrival	Elapsed time			Handicap* time		Position*
				D	H	M	D	H	
1	*Pen Duick II*	Eric Tabarly	19/6	27	03	56	21	23	1
2	*Gipsy Moth III*	Francis Chichester	22/6	29	23	57	22	18	2
3	*Akka*	Val Howells	25/6	32	18	08	24	07	3
4	*Lively Lady*	Alec Rose	29/6	36	17	30	27	09	5
5	*Jester*	Blondie Hasler	30/6	37	22	05	25	04	4
6	*Stardrift*	Bill Howell	30/6	38	03	23	27	12	6
7	*Rehu Moana*	David Lewis	30/6	38	12	04			*
8	*Ilala*	Mike Ellison	8/7	46	06	26	34	20	9
9	*Golif*	Jean Lacombe	8/7	46	07	05	30	00	7
10	*Vanda Caelea*	Bob Bunker	12/7	49	18	45	32	22	8
11	*Misty Miller*	Michael Butterfield	15/7	53	00	05			*
12	*Ericht 2*	Geoffrey Chaffey	22/7	60	11	15	42	23	10
13	*Folatre*	Derek Kelsall	24/7	61	14	04			*
14	*Marco Polo*	Axel Pederson	26/7	63	13	30	44	21	11

Final placings in 1964 Observer Singlehanded

* Multihulls not eligible for the handicap award. *Akka* was delayed at start and put into Ireland for repairs. *Misty Miller* and *Ericht 2* put into Azores for repairs. *Marco Polo* left Plymouth 10.58 26 May. *Folatre* returned to Plymouth damaged and left again noon 19 June. *Tammie Norie* retired.

sailor, a hell of a fine chap and tough as old boots.'

From the second race there were two lessons to be learned. The first is obvious: a boat designed and built specially for singlehanded ocean sailing has an enormous advantage over other yachts merely adapted for the Observer race. If it happens also to be the biggest boat in the race the odds in its favour become overwhelming. It was a lesson taught again four years later.

Secondly, the multihulls proved that they could compete on equal terms. All three finished, albeit well down the field, but David Lewis's *Rehu Moana* did beat the winning time of the previous race (he took $38\frac{1}{2}$ days to cross), while Kelsall's second attempt in 35 days was the fifth fastest solo crossing ever at that time.

For the second race a handicap award was instituted. It was based on the formula $\dfrac{\sqrt{L}+2}{10}$ where L is as that used in the then RORC formula. Multihulls were excluded. It did not prove very much, except that Hasler's *Jester* had done well for her length by catching all those easterlies on the high northern route.

The best and most sporting summing-up of the '64 race came again from the father-figure himself. In August, when even Pederson had staggered into Newport (he took 63 days), Blondie Hasler wrote in *The Observer*: 'Eric Tabarly's win in the lovely *Pen Duick II* delighted me for two reasons – he was a foreign entrant in a British event, and his boat was the first ever to be designed specifically for the race. This is exactly what I hoped would happen when we first planned the thing . . . . The boat was built on a very small budget, and Eric's performance in getting her to the Brenton Reef in 27 days, in spite of an unserviceable vane steering gear, must rank very near the summit of singlehanded sailing.'

6 The 1968 Race

If the 1964 Observer Singlehanded marked the race's graduation to an international event, the 1968 contest conferred the doctorate. There were more boats from more countries, in a greater variety of sizes and shapes, with more commercial sponsors and more contracts for the sailors to provide reports to newspapers and magazines.

But with the growth of numbers and the huge increase in public interest came other qualities which saddened some of the veterans. All the new sponsorship meant commercial pressures, of course. Many of the '68 sailors were striving hard to win not just for themselves but for the firms that had put up the money – and opinions were very divided about that. The money showed in the fleet, too. The yachts were much, much bigger and the number that had been specially built to win the race had leapt up.

It was still the toughest, longest, and loneliest race in the world, but now it had acquired an extra hard edge of competitiveness that went deep beneath the superficial bonhomie among competitors as they met in Plymouth the week before the starting date of Saturday 1 June 1968.

Fortunately, there were still plenty of entrants who wanted to race just for the sake of having taken part. There were a couple of Swedish boats of less than 20 feet overall, for example, and dear old *Jester* was there again, though not with Blondie Hasler at the helm. He had sold the Folkboat to Michael Richey, who ran the Institute of Navigation (now the Royal Institute) and was well known as a fine navigator, especially in offshore racing.

But though *Jester* kept the Hasler spirit in the race, it was disappointing to find none of the 1960 veteran sailors in the lists. In fact, only Eric Tabarly and Bill Howell of the 15 starters in the 1964 race were ready to go again, and they both had new boats. In several ways these two singlehanders were very typical of the 'new look' of the Observer Singlehanded. First, they were foreign entrants – Tabarly is the archetypal Frenchman and Howell is Australian and proud of it, for all his many years' residence in London. There were 19 other foreign starters in 1968, against only 14 sailors from the UK.

Next, they had bigger boats than four years earlier. Tabarly's new craft was a vast trimaran 67 feet long (it's now 70 foot) with a 35 foot beam – a sailing tennis court, some- body called it. Howell had a new catamaran, just a foot shorter than Tabarly's winner of 1964. *Golden Cockerel* measures 43 feet overall with a 17 feet beam.

Everybody else had bigger boats, too. If Tabarly had decided to sail in *Pen Duick II* again, he would have been tenth in order of size, for there were no less than eight yachts of over 50 feet in length entered, and another of 45 feet.

Third, both Tabarly and Howell had gone for multihulls – and 1968 was a vintage year for them. Of 35 entrants, 13 had two or three hulls – a reflection, perhaps, of the stir caused by the multihull success in the 1966 Observer/Express Round Britain Race.

Finally, Tabarly and Howell were, in varying degrees, sponsored. Howell's catamaran was called *Golden Cockerel* because that is the symbol of the Courage brewery, which provided him with cash for fittings on the boat and a few liquid rations too. Tabarly had no direct sponsorship of that kind, but as a serving naval lieutenant seconded to the Ministry of Sport he did have his living expenses paid by the French government. Contracts with magazines and commercial radio paid for the new yacht.

Just how much sponsorship the other boats received is impossible to put into finite terms. Some competitors gleaned minimal help with a small amount of cash, paid time off, or maybe just some piece of equipment. Others had virtually all their costs underwritten by a sponsor. A look down the names of the competing boats gives a quick indication of which sailors had achieved the best pay-offs.

Geoffrey Williams' *Sir Thomas Lipton* was the most fancied of the British entrants. It was specially designed for the race by Robert Clark and derived its name from the fact that it was paid for by Allied Suppliers, the grocery group that encompasses the Lipton's stores and brand of tea. A 57 foot ketch, the yacht looked as though it would give Tabarly's monster multihull a run for its money.

Leslie Williams (no relation) also found a sponsor to foot the bill. Cutty Sark whisky were the benefactors, *Spirit of Cutty Sark* the Gallant 53 foot sloop that resulted. Like Tabarly, Williams was a serving lieutenant in the Navy. More people hoped this was a good omen than simply the makers of Cutty Sark Scotch.

Actually, there was a distinctly alcoholic look to the list of runners. Apart from Howell's *Golden Cockerel* and Williams' boat, there were two other contenders with booze makers for backers. Captain Martin Minter-Kemp of the Welch Fusiliers had entered Tim Powell's 45 foot trimaran that won the '66 Round Britain. Then she was known as *Toria*, but financial help from the House of Gancia (an Italian sparkling wine) dictated a change to *Gancia Girl*.

Colin Forbes had one of the smaller trimarans – just 33 feet overall. Her name was *Startled Faun* and her backers another brewery – Watneys. They hoped for, and got, a first class film of the race for their money.

One other feature of the 1968 race was novel – Ladbrokes ran a book on it. That's a clear indication of public interest, if you like. And though the British press had concerned itself mainly with home contenders, the bookmakers were quick to see the threats from overseas. Tabarly was favourite, of course. As winner last time and now the skipper with the biggest boat in the fleet, he was bound to be the man to beat. But *Pen Duick IV* was far from proven – she sailed for the first time only on 11 May – and some of the wiser seamen in Plymouth thought odds of 3 to 1 were a bit fierce, even though a Frenchman was heard to say 'Untried boat? Ha! Eric could win the race at 20 knots on a piece of bread.'

Second in the bookie's list came three boats of impressively big dimensions. The French yachting editor Alain Gliksman had entered a 58 foot ketch called *Raph*; Alex Carozzo, the man they called 'Italy's Chichester', was to sail a 53 foot ketch-rigged catamaran called *San Giorgio*, and Britain's Eric Willis was matching his expert seamanship to a newly built 50 foot trimaran named *Coila*. They all received odds of 8 to 1.

The eventual winner, *Sir Thomas Lipton*, was quoted at 10 to 1, along with *Golden Cockerel* and a 50 foot trimaran *Yaksha* entered by Frenchman Joan de Kat. South African Bruce Dalling and his ketch *Voortrekker* were quoted at 12 to 1, while two multihulls, *Gancia Girl* and Sandy Munro's catamaran *Ocean Highlander* were given 14 to 1 chances.

At 16 to 1 were listed what should have been the outsiders, but there was still a slightly reluctant feeling among yachting men that one of the boats quoted at those odds might spring a surprise. Her name was *Cheers* and she was easily the oddest-looking yacht in the fleet, even including the monstrous *Pen Duick IV* and the Frenchman Waquet's minimal trimaran *Tamouré*. *Cheers* was a proa – two hulls 40 feet long and two unstayed masts on the weather hull. She didn't tack, she changed ends. To go about you reversed the sails and went off with what were your sterns now your prows (they had quite a problem deciding where to break the bottle when they named her).

If the bookmakers were not quite sure where to place *Cheers* on their lists, they had no hesitation about another boat which was attracting much of the Press attention in Plymouth. That was *Koala III*, a 39 foot trimaran being sailed by an attractive 26-year-old German secretary called Edith Baumann – the first woman ever to enter an Observer Single-handed. She had been sailing less than a year. The yachting men shook their heads and the bookmakers put *Koala III* bottom of the list – the rank outsider at 100 to 1.

There were other good stories for the journalists at Plymouth. Stephen Pakenham, the vicar of Apuldram and Donnington, in Sussex, for example. He had exchanged his dog collar for a sailing sweater and was off to America in a 32 foot ketch called *Rob Roy*. And Brian Cooke, sub-manager of the Westminster Bank's Poole branch, who was setting out in the 32 foot sloop *Opus*.

David Pyle's boat caught some technical eyes, too. She was *Atlantis III*, a 27 foot sloop that Pyle had built himself on the 'egg-box' principle – marine ply frames are set in the hull to provide the sort of strength derived from this method in aircraft and ship construction and to ensure watertight bulkheads along the boat.

For the rest, it was the kind of motley collection of cruising yachts you might find in any small port. The unifying factor here was that every skipper was determined to sail solo to America, no matter how long it took. For some, it was obviously going to be six weeks or more before that ambition was achieved, for there were eight yachts of less than 30 feet in the

Three Cheers in a stiff breeze. Tom Follett shows how well Dick Newick's design works during trials in the West Indies

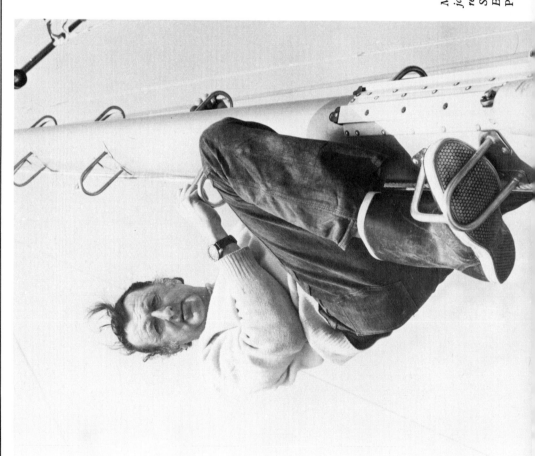

Murray Sayle is the adventurous kind of journalist who believes in being there to get the real story. If he had not sailed in the Observer Singlehanded he would have been halfway up Everest, covering the expedition there
Photo: Bob Salmon

You can tell it's big just by the number of flags.
Gerard Dijkstra seems quite imperturbed by the
71 foot length of Second Life at her launching
Photo: Bryn Campbell

Michael Richey sailed Jester, the only yacht to compete in all four Observer Singlehanded races – twice when owned by the race's instigator Blondie Hasler and twice by Richey
Photo: Bryn Campbell

Captain Pat Chilton is a retired Fleet Air Arm test pilot, so navigation aboard his sloop Mary Kate of Arun was no problem
Photo: Bob Salmon

Eric Sumner and Francette not only were the first entrants for the 1972 race – for a long time they were the only entrants. Sumner is proud of his sail number 1. He reported by radio to the Sea Cadets – he is the Corps' official entry
Photo: Ian Cook

*Jean-Marie Vidal attracted little press attention
before the race, but the French yachting papers
were quietly confident that he would do well with
the big trimaran Cap 33
Photo: P. Sully Azéma*

Wild Rocket, a 63 foot schooner, was sighted in the evening after the start. She had apparently moved into second place at that time, but blew out her sails and then put back into Plymouth to repair them

Richard Clifford's Shamaal is one of the well-known Contessa 26s built at Lymington. Clifford's sail in the Observer Singlehanded was a kind of busman's holiday, for he is a Marines officer with the Special Boat Service, and spends most of his time on or under the water
Photo: Neil Libbert

Claus Hehner sailed his 35-foot sloop Mex for the second time. In 1968 he had come fourteenth in 41½ days, then followed up with a heroic direct voyage in the Trans-Pacific race Photo: Bob Salmon

Zbigniew Puchalski has a great respect for Sir Francis Chichester – he named his boat Miranda after the self-steering gear which Chichester used on his Gipsy Moth III to win the first Observer Singlehanded. Miranda is an old boat, but she looks well under Puchalski's skilled care
Photo: Chris Smith

Martin Minter-Kemp surveys the underside of his long slim hull while Strongbow is being built at Bristol. It represents the advanced thinking of designer Michael Pipe, creator of Slithy Tove

Photo: Chris Smith

Strongbow proved early in her trials that she was capable of slicing her slim hull through the water at 20 knots or more in the right conditions.

Here Martin Minter-Kemp has her moving well in a good breeze
Photo: Chris Smith

The arrows on the bows of Andrew Spedding's
Summersong soon pointed towards Newport.
As he said at the pre-race party, 'It's out to the
Eddystone then turn right, isn't it?'
Photo: Neil Libbert

Sir Francis Chichester and the latest in the Gipsy Moth series. This one is designed by Robert Clark and had already covered 18,000 miles with Sir Francis in sole command before the race started
Photo: Chris Smith

Alain Colas acquired Pen Duick IV from Eric Tabarly, winner of the 1964 Observer Singlehanded, after Tabarly had been forced to retire her from the 1968 race. Colas then proved that she was fit for an ocean crossing by sailing her 9600 miles alone

Photo: Chris Smith

lists, and another seven that would have qualified for the trophy for first boat home under 35 feet if it had been offered then.

They looked small enough tied up safely alongside the ocean greyhounds in Millbay Docks. How well would they cope with the big seas and wide horizons of the Western Ocean?

It was a question asked by thousands on that bleak Saturday morning as 35 boats made their way to the start line in Plymouth Sound. Despite grey skies, low winds, and depressing rain, the crowds turned out again, but their brave persistence was not well rewarded. In minimal wind the fleet crept across the line and made for the Channel. Stephen Pakenham made a little progress by rowing; Edith Baumann decided there was just not enough wind and put back into Plymouth. Tabarly edged *Pen Duick IV* into a narrow lead and Geoffrey Williams struggled grimly to get every ounce of effort out of *Sir Thomas Lipton*.

Williams had not been distinguished by his ability to make friends at the start of the race. The quiet Cornishman had experienced some difficulty getting his boat to Plymouth on time, and when he did arrive, was towed to Mashford's yard across at Cremyll rather than into the dock with the others. He was worried about a leak through the fairing between hull and keel on *Sir Thomas Lipton*, he reported. It wasn't cracked, in fact, and the Race Committee gave him a 12-hour penalty for late arrival.

Pakenham noticed Williams' distance particularly. 'I felt embarrassed; should one have tried to break through the wall which Geoffrey seemed to have built around himself?' he asked later, in his book *Separate Horizons*. But in Williams' own book there is some rationalisation of his remove. 'I dreaded the weeks of sleepless action that were to come and longed with all my heart to stop the clocks, to put off the awful hour and give myself time to rest and prepare my mind ... this race would stretch me continuously, never letting me relax, never letting me forget the hundreds of people who had put energy, money, and trust in *Lipton*, never letting his bows look away from Newport, USA.' Interesting ammunition for the anti-sponsorship lobby.

Williams had also hogged the press limelight, and alienated the sympathies of some traditionalists, by announcing that he would have the benefit of recom-

mended courses radioed to him, based on a computer assessment of his position in relation to the detailed weather map available in London.

Was it cricket? Some thought it acceptable within the Hasler philosophy of trying to make ocean passages faster and more comfortable for solo sailers. Others thought that if man or machine were working out your course for you it was no longer strictly a singlehanded voyage. Williams himself was not even sure if it would make much difference. 'Although computer course planning might give me a tactical advantage on only one or two days,' he wrote, 'this could win the race.' But when the computer experiment started to throw up problems – he had to have a full range of navigation instruments installed, plus a powerful radio set with all its attendant wiring, batteries, generating plant, and fuel – he was inclined to abandon the whole thing. 'Then I would wonder if I was discarding a race-winning trump.'

For the sake of dramatic simplification one could say it was certainly the race-winning trump, for it helped Geoffrey Williams to avoid a hurricane-strength storm that hit the front runners in the race ten days out. But a contest between 35 boats spread out across hundreds of miles of ocean is not that simple. Fate played a few other cards before Geoffrey Williams won the last trick that put him first into Newport.

To begin with, there was a double blow to French hopes. Joan de Kat suffered a broken forestay on *Yaksha* and had to put into Alderney for repairs. There were plenty of 'I told you sos' in Plymouth, for eyebrows had been twitching furiously at the sight of this home-built trimaran. It seemed to acknowledge its own weaknesses by the proliferation of rigging wire in every direction.

More serious was the news that Tabarly was in trouble. Just 36 hours after the start he was back in Plymouth with considerable damage. After missing one ship by less than 30 yards he went below to brew some coffee – perhaps to settle his nerves – and just 15 minutes later ran into another. 'There was a tremendous crash ... it was a small freighter and it was anchored when I ran into it at about 15 knots.' There was a gash in his starboard float and a deal of rigging damage. By the time it was all repaired and *Pen Duick IV* hared out of Plymouth Sound again it was Tuesday night. By Wednesday morning the favourite was certainly out of the race. The hastily prepared trimaran was shaking its steering gear to pieces at speed and Tabarly never sailed further than the Scillies.

Already the retirements outnumbered any previous race. Egon Hienemann put his sloop *Aye-Aye* into Falmouth on Monday and dropped out with steering gear problems. Commander Waquet's trimaran *Tamouré* sailed straight off to Brest – he couldn't attempt the crossing because he relied on navigational help from passing Air France planes, and they had gone on strike.

Other retirements came at regular intervals. Robert Wingate tried three times to get started in *Zeevalk*, but eventually had to give up in Plymouth on 19 June. Michael Pulsford had a similar history with his home-built trimaran *White Ghost*. They gave it up at Plymouth on 14 July. The Swede William Wallin tried for five days to put up with the cold of the North Atlantic before he shivered to a stop.

Lionel Paillard suffered a broken mast on *La Delirante* and headed back to France, while Carozzo's *San Giorgio* limped into Falmouth with a rudder damaged by a large piece of driftwood. Sandy Munro had perhaps the hardest luck of all. In order to report to the *Daily Express* he had installed radio equipment and converted his backstays into a transmitting aerial. He wanted insulators capable of taking a 5 ton strain. Somehow he got ones rated at 5,000 lbs (2·2 tons). The first strong wind abaft the beam snapped them and collapsed the mast at the lower shrouds. He sailed back under jury rig thickening the Atlantic air with some ripe expletives about chandlers!

Silvia II was also dismasted, but her French skipper, André Foëzon, was not dismayed. He put back to Plymouth for repair and started again on 12 June, to finish remarkably quickly just over 29 days later – a superb achievement with a 36 foot sloop that would have given him the handicap prize by a street if he could have done it first time. Foëzon was the Kelsall of the 1968 race, in fact.

At the end of the first week a pattern had started to emerge among the leaders. On the direct (great circle) route it looked as though Bruce Dalling had nosed ahead of the field, with Gliksman's *Raph* close at hand and Geoffrey Williams within striking distance. Not far behind came Leslie Williams and

Bill Howell, with the Australian able to make up some distance on Williams because the British sailor was having trouble with the arm he had injured in a fall a week before the start.

Down to the south, *Cheers* and Tom Follett were making good progress towards the Azores, having determined to follow that route. Follett actually completed 1,000 miles in the first seven days, with *Cheers* whipping along through gentle seas under a fair wind.

Three days later the scene changed. A deep depression swept across the Atlantic intensifying as it went. It hit the leading boats on the 10th and worsened steadily. On the 11th Bruce Dalling's *Voortrekker* was lying ahull for 13 hours in winds of force 11 or 10 – around 60 knots. Leslie Williams lost 29 hours and Bill Howell's *Golden Cockerel* lay ahull for 34 hours. Cooke reported a knockdown to *Opus* and Minter-Kemp also lost more than a whole day.

This was the crucial period of the race, for on the 11th *Sir Thomas Lipton* moved into the lead and was never headed again. Why? Because Williams had been advised to move north by his computer course planners and had just skirted the worst of the depression. He had a hard day on the 10th, but on the 11th he was making good progress again. Ian Slater, the man in charge of the computer in London, wrote later that he thought the diversion had given Williams a lead of 300 miles over his nearest rivals. When he arrived in Newport, *Lipton's* skipper said 'I think I made up perhaps 200 or 300 miles on *Golden Cockerel* and on *Spirit of Cutty Sark* at this time.'

Going north was the only way to avoid this storm belt. It reached right down to those boats going by the Azores route and even to Michael Richey in *Jester*, who was determined to see if going the long way round by the southern trade winds route would pay any dividends.

On the 12th disaster struck yet another French competitor. Marc Cuiklinski's *Ambrima* was dismasted and the rudder torn off. She was taken in tow by a Spanish vessel but sank before making port. Piazzini also retired about this time, having sailed *Gunther III* back to Plymouth with a broken mast step.

But the most dramatic moments of the third week concerned one more of the French contingent – the eccentric but likeable Joan de Kat and his equally eccentric *Yaksha*. They had set out again from the Channel Islands on 9 June, heading for the high northern route. On the morning of Tuesday the 18th a civilian aircraft picked up a distress message from trimaran number 43. The Frenchman had apparently lost a rudder, a mast, and one float and was abandoning ship. There started a massive rescue operation that involved the ships and planes of six nations. It ended with de Kat being found by an RAF Shackleton and then picked up safely from his dinghy by a Norwegian bulk carrier on her way to Latvia.

By this time – 20 June – the leaders were getting close to the American coast. *Sir Thomas Lipton* was south of Newfoundland, heading towards Sable Island. Gliksman's *Raph* had passed through Williams' wake the day before, heading for St John in Newfoundland with a damaged rudder. He set out again on 23 June, but had to give up because the boat was still not right.

On that day the leaders were converging on Newport. Geoffrey Williams had a problem on the 21st when a jammed halliard on his mizzen prevented him from tacking away from the coast of Nova Scotia. By the time he was able to climb the mast and free it he was virtually committed to a course which would take him north of the Nantucket light, though in fact his sailing instructions should have been amended at the pre-race briefing to read 'thence to Newport passing south of Nantucket light vessel.'

When those in Newport realised from his radio calls that Williams was passing north of the light they told him that he was taking the wrong course. He replied that his instructions read 'pass south of Nantucket—full stop', and asked for guidance. Colonel Odling-Smee, the race official in Newport, had a tricky decision to make. Should he force Williams to go about and sail back round Nantucket light? He decided that Williams could follow his instructions as written, so *Sir Thomas Lipton* continued on a course north of the light and just south of the four fathom mark on the Nantucket shoals. With a 40 knot wind speeding him home, Williams hustled his yacht across the frothing shoals towards Brenton Reef and the finishing line.

It was a momentous decision for Odling-Smee and one that was the subject of many a post mortem as more and more boats arrived at Newport.

Williams wrote in his book *Sir Thomas Lipton Wins* that he thought it would have added only an hour and a half to his time if he had gone south of the light. Bruce Dalling in *Voortrekker* followed him into Newport 17 hours later. As Williams was already under a 12-hour penalty he had precious little in hand.

But the South African, though bitterly disappointed at being beaten into second place, refused to protest against the first boat home, even when a member of the Voortrekker Trust that had backed him sent a fiery telegram about *Sir Thomas Lipton* having sailed against the rules. It blew over, inevitably, though Dalling never quite lost his disappointment. When I asked him about it three years later, at the time of the 1971 Admiral's Cup series, his anxiety to drop the subject quickly bore witness to the scar on his memory.

Also disappointed were the happy band who make up the Project Cheers team. Their deceptively fast proa, guided by the immense experience of Tom Follett, had crossed the line third a few hours behind *Voortrekker*. The original design had paid off, even if it had not taken victory from the big monohulls. Surprisingly, *Cheers* had sailed 384 fewer miles than *Lipton*, despite taking the Azores route, because favourable winds allowed Follett to sail a more direct course. On one day he actually covered 225 nautical miles – better than any other boat in the race.

With these three home, the focus shifted to the second group of yachts approaching the American seaboard. They were lead by Leslie Williams in *Spirit of Cutty Sark*, with Bill Howell's *Golden Cockerel* not far behind. Then came *Opus*, with Brian Cooke making extremely good time for his boat's meagre length of 32 feet, Martin Minter-Kemp in *Gancia Girl*, and Noel Bevan's *Myth of Malham*. They finished in that order.

But the attention of the world was not wholly concentrated on Rhode Island during that week. Even as the leaders sliced away the last few miles of the momentous voyage the alarms were out in a far distant part of the ocean. Edith Baumann and her little dog Schatz caught the tail end of that storm which had played such a dramatic part in Geoffrey Williams' success. A couple of vital stays between main hull and outriggers snapped and it looked as though the boat would break up.

A large freighter saw one of her distress flares, came to within 200 yards and then steamed away for some inexplicable reason, but a Mayday call was picked up and resulted in Edith being spotted by a US Air Force Hercules. This attracted a French research vessel to a gallant rescue, but unfortunately at the loss of *Koala III*, complete with the German secretary's party dress specially packed for the post-race festivities in Newport.

There were plenty of them, of course, though for the first time in the series the equivocal way in which the race had been won did cast a shadow over some of the fun. Dalling magnanimously dismissed as negligible the advantage Geoffrey Williams might have gained by being computer-assisted, but, more significantly, he refused to discuss the Nantucket light business.

Four years later the arguments go on. Just how far

north of the light was Williams? Could he really have gone about and rounded the light with the loss of only one and half hours? One or two of the competitors who followed Williams and Dalling home thought the time saved on *Sir Thomas Lipton*'s voyage could have been as much as two whole days – not only because the course across the shoals cut a corner but also because it continued close to the New England coast, with its more favourable currents and winds. If they had been as close as Dalling in such circumstances they would certainly have protested.

The lessons of the 1968 race are many. Perhaps the most obvious one is that the rules should be made absolutely explicit to every competitor and then rigidly enforced. The fact that Geoffrey Williams sidestepped the official rulings both at the start of the race and again near the end may or may not have

Place	Yacht	Crew	Elapsed time			Handicap			Position
			D	H	M	D	H	M	
1	*Sir Thomas Lipton*	Geoffrey Williams	25	20	33	*			
2	*Voortrekker*	Bruce Dalling	26	13	42	22	16	51	1
3	*Cheers*	Tom Follett	27	00	13	*			
4	*Spirit of Cutty Sark*	Leslie Williams	29	10	17	25	02	44	4
5	*Golden Cockerel*	Bill Howell	31	16	24	*			
6	*Opus*	Brian Cooke	34	08	23	24	16	14	3
7	*Gancia Girl*	Martin Minter-Kemp	34	13	15	*			
8	*Myth of Malham*	Noel Bevan	36	01	41	28	11	01	8
9	*Maxine*	Bertrand de Castelbajac	37	13	47	27	08	36	6
10	*Maguelonne*	Jean-Yves Terlain	38	09	10	27	18	17	7
11	*Dogwatch*	Nigel Burgess	38	12	13	27	06	20	5
12	*Silvia II*	André Foëzon	40	00	16	29	12	29	9
13	*Fione*	Bertil Enbom	40	14	13	24	14	13	2
14	*Mex*	Claus Hehne	41	10	46	32	00	04	11
15	*Rob Roy*	Stephen Pakenham	42	03	49	30	10	20	10
16	*Startled Faun*	Colin Forbes	45	10	08	*			
17	*Amistad*	Bernard Rodriquez	47	18	05	*			
18	*Goodwin II*	Ake Mattson	50	19	48	*			
19	*Jester*	Michael Richey	57	10	40	37	19	43	12

Final placings in 1968 Observer Singlehanded

* Multihulled boats were not eligible for the Handicap Trophy.

† *Sir Thomas Lipton* did not have a handicap as she was not presented for scrutineering before the race.

Goodwin II finished 18th but was not placed, since she was disqualified under rule 21 (taking on supplies during the race).

affected his ability to get to Newport before anybody else. The fact that the officials of the Royal Western Yacht Club, themselves amateur yachtsmen, reacted generously on each occasion indicates that the race remained a sporting contest, despite the considerably increased commercial pressures. Nevertheless, it is significant that in the rules for the 1972 race the course (south of the Nantucket light, it goes without saying) and the ruling against prearranged radio transmissions for the use of individual competitors are very clearly set down.

Lesson number two: an unconventional design of boat can win, or come very close to winning the Observer Singlehanded. Tom Follett and *Cheers* finished third very close behind Dalling's *Voortrekker*, having proved convincingly that a lightweight proa helmed by an expert seaman could give away 10 feet in overall length, sail the Azores route, and still be close up at the finish. It was a triumph for the energetic and original minds behind Project Cheers.

Third, multihulls of good design can hold their own on a transatlantic crossing. The first three took third, fifth, and seventh places. Against that, of course, must be considered the opposite argument that the failure rate among the multihulls was high,

too. Of the 13 that started, only five reached Newport and two of the three sinkings were trimarans. But it is important to stress that phrase 'of good design', for multihull development is still in its early stages and there have to be failures among the misconceived designs to point the way towards success.

And, for the record, it should be pointed out that another trimaran – Eric Willis's *Coila* – was going fine for Newport when a strange bug struck down her crew, so that he had to be rescued by paramedics. The boat itself was making very good progress.

Last, there was a salutary lesson for the French contingent. After Eric Tabarly's runaway win in 1964 there was more than a hint of complacency about their confidence of victory in this one. Yet the big boats of Tabarly and Gliksman failed to stay the course, de Kat's trimaran sank and the first Frenchman home – Bertrand de Castelbajac, who finished ninth – got there in a British-designed boat. The first French-designed yacht to finish was next in the list – *Maguelonne*, a small sloop sailed by a man of whom we were to hear rather a lot four years later. His name was Jean-Yves Terlain.

7 The Entry – 1972

Early in 1972 I drew a graph. It was a very simple graph, for it merely related the number of starters to each of the three previous Observer Singlehanded races and projected a figure for the 1972 event. The result was a beautifully consistent curve, sweeping up through 5 (1960), 15 ('64), and 35 ('68) to pass through the '72 mark at around 60.

But despite the mathematical logic of it, I could find few people who believed that as many as 60 solo sailors would want to set out for America on the 17th of June, 1972. Quite apart from any reasonably sensible doubts that the world actually contained that number of singlehanders keen enough to want to make the trip, there were a number of other factors which seemed to be working against the possibility of a starting fleet of 60. Indeed, to many it seemed probable that the number leaving Plymouth that Saturday would be far less than four years earlier.

After all, wasn't sponsorship much more difficult to find? Both because of the new ruling about names of boats, and because the number of commercial firms with that sort of money to spend seemed to have diminished anyway. Blondie Hasler told me that he was often asked by aspiring adventurers how to get money for their projects, and his advice was to forget about the big companies – they had all turned down hundreds of similar requests – and try to find some moneyed eccentric, perhaps a laird presiding over a huge estate in the highlands of Scotland, who might be stimulated by the adventurous motivation of an unusual project and provide the modern equivalent of artistic patronage of old.

And wasn't the new qualifying rule going to thin out the ranks? Previously, entrants were required to have sailed 500 miles solo, but not necessarily in the boat they intended to use in the race. Now both boat and sailor were required to have completed the 500 miles. And since entries closed on 17 April, two months before the start, this meant that last-minute yacht deliveries were out – boat and crew had to be fit to make a 500 mile cruise before that crucial mid-April date, in many cases in near-winter conditions.

The point of the new ruling was, of course, to prevent any ill-prepared boats coming to the line. If the yacht had completed a 500 mile solo sail a full two months before the start date, the chances were that it would be in a fit condition to face Atlantic conditions. Or if it were not, there remained a couple of months to get it properly sorted out before the off.

So the sceptics were not surprised when, despite a flood of enquiries for information and entry forms to the Royal Western, firm starters were few at first. A year before the start, more than 200 enquiries had arrived in Plymouth and eventually that number was to rise to well over 300, from more than 30 countries. Yet at that time there was just a solitary firm entry.

But Captain Terence Shaw, the Royal Western's Sailing Secretary, was not dismayed. He had made his own assessment of the odds in favour of a definite entry, and he nodded wisely when I told him of my graph. Then, as the months passed, he spoke more confidently of around 60 starters. A few weeks before the April deadline that seemed to be wishful thinking, then a last frantic rush and some odd diversions piled up the numbers. And the last sail number to be allocated was 59.

It is interesting here to speculate about 1976. If my graph line is continued onwards and upwards, it passes through the 1976 mark at around 100.

Those 59 definite entries represented the most motley collection of yachts and yachtsmen ever to join the lists for a race in the history of sail. The smallest was a little 19 foot sloop, the biggest a huge 128 foot schooner (again, as in every race in the series, people were asking if one man could possibly handle such a vast craft). The slimmest beam was 6·2 feet; the broadest 35. The newest boat entered the water in the spring of 1972; the oldest was launched in 1908. The youngest competitor was 26; the oldest the indomitable Sir Francis Chichester, going for his third Observer Singlehanded at the age of 70.

The entrants came from 12 different countries, with France's 14 applicants the nearest challenge to the British total of 23. Then came America with five starters and Italy with four. One of the really dramatic moments in the build-up to the '72 race was when the first ever entry from an Iron Curtain country arrived. Eventually Poland mustered three starters and Czechoslovakia one. Entries from Australia (two), West Germany (three), Holland (one), Belgium (one), Switzerland (one), and Sweden (one) completed the list.

The biggest ever number of starters were to compete for the longest ever list of trophies. *The Observer* had decided to offer four trophies instead of the previous two (outright winner and handicap for monohulls). The additions were for the fastest crossing made by any yacht measuring 35 feet or less, and a handicap trophy for the multihullers.

In fact, the number of multihull yachts entered as a proportion of the total had dropped sharply. In 1968 there were 13 multihulls in the fleet of 35 yachts that left Plymouth. In the 1972 entry list there were just six trimarans and two catamarans.

One trophy was contested by only five of the yachts – that awarded by the Ida Lewis Yacht Club for the first American boat home.

For the handicap prizes the Royal Western Yacht Club relied on the system used for the 1968 race – what Blondie Hasler, in an article for *The Observer*, called 'the best in the world, since no designer can possibly find a loophole in it, while its scope embraces every known and unknown sailing vessel. It consists of a number of experienced and totally incorruptible members of the Race Committee who look at each boat, sometimes take a few measurements, and then decide out of the top of their heads how fast it ought to sail the course. They then award it the appropriate handicap factor.'

In the same article Hasler assessed the chances of the various contenders for the different trophies, and it is not without significance that he started with the multihull yachts. For, despite their small numbers, they made a formidable bunch – with six of the eight boats likely to be among the front runners.

The multihull attack was spearheaded by a Frenchman and an American. Alain Colas brought Tabarly's 1968 boat, the huge trimaran *Pen Duick IV*. In the four years since the 1968 disaster, Colas had sorted out all the problems and put in some impressively fast solo sailing. In fact, the boat was sailed half way round the world virtually singlehanded in order to enter the race, because Colas used to be a Professor of French in Sydney and he brought *Pen Duick IV* from there to Britanny.

For much of the journey he had a crew member who provided little more than company. Then from La Réunion, near Mauritius, he brought *Pen Duick* the 9,600 miles home alone, averaging 150 miles a day and actually totting up 305 miles on one particularly good day – 64 days of very fast sailing in all conditions.

From across the Atlantic came an equally impressive challenge. Tom Follett entered again, and once more his yacht was the outcome of that fruitful association between himself, backer Jim Morris, and designer Dick Newick. This time Newick had produced a sleek trimaran, 46 feet long, and the team had settled for the fairly obvious name of *Three Cheers*. Yawl rigged, she displaced only 3 tons and was sufficiently well balanced for Follett to manage without self-steering gear – as he had done with *Cheers* four years earlier. Before the start, Follett sailed *Three Cheers* the 4,000 miles from the Virgin Islands to Plymouth in 24 days – and then complained of being held up in the Bay of Biscay!

Supporting Colas in the French bid for the overall trophy, or at least for the multihull handicap prize, was Jean-Marie Vidal, who entered a 53 foot trimaran called *Cap 33* – and managed to fix for himself the sail number 33. This was one of the entries that came in the late rush and little was known about her in Britain before the boats assembled in Plymouth. But Alain Gliksman, the French yachting journalist who himself entered in the slim and swift *Toucan*, told me in May that he thought both Colas and Vidal should be in the first ten, maybe the first five.

Two British designed trimarans promised to give the foreigners a run for their money. Both came from the board of Derek Kelsall and they were nearly identical in size. John Beswick's *Leen Valley Venturer* measured a few inches less than Philip Weld's *Trumpeter*. Both had proved fast and seaworthy during the 1970 Round Britain race. Beswick, a garage owner from near Nottingham, built *Venturer* himself – 'it was the longest and largest craft I could build in my back garden' – and was justifiably proud of her solid construction. He boasted to me that the only bilge pump he had needed since the boat was built had been a sponge.

Philip Weld is a New Englander, a newspaper publisher from Massachusetts. Always a multihull enthusiast, his greatest achievement before the 1972

Observer Singlehanded was third place in the 1970 Round Britain. In an interview in *Sail* magazine about his preparation for the race, Weld stated his own version of the Hasler philosophy. 'How long it is going to take for the average sailor to care about getting there more safely, faster, and in more comfort, I really don't know. But as more and more people go to sea and discover how good a trimaran is, I think you'll see more conversions.

'People talk about comfort. Well, *Trumpeter* is very comfortable in anything up to 35 knots. Over 35 knots I'm not sure what 40 foot boat is going to be comfortable.'

In the same article Weld had some very pertinent comments to make about the race in general, saying that crossing the Atlantic, or the Pacific for that matter, was no longer extraordinary, though most solo crossings were at a leisurely pace. 'But to make the passage quickly and in safety is quite another matter, and this is the fascinating part of any single-handed race. It is a delicate combination of physical and intellectual demands.

'I have a hunch that this year's Transatlantic Race will be won by a boat that crosses the finish line in less than 500 hours, which is 20 days, 20 hours, and is five days faster than *Sir Thomas Lipton's* passage four years ago . . .' What appeals to me, and I think to most of us who sail in it, is that there is a big element of luck, a big element of preparedness and equally big elements that call for great physical and mental endurance. There are few sporting events that can match it.'

Equally convinced that a multihull is the right kind of boat for ocean passages is Bill Howell, who again entered *Golden Cockerel* for the '72 race, and again claimed the number 13 sail which he had taken to fifth place in 1968. But *Golden Cockerel* had changed quite a lot since 1968. Howell had dispensed with the mizzen mast, which he found largely useless during the transatlantic passage, and lightened the 43 foot catamaran considerably. One important weight saving was made by taking out the long range radio transmitter, with all its batteries, charging gear, and fuel requirements. For Howell had decided this time that he would sail entirely under his own auspices. Indeed, just as the entry list closed, he obtained permission to change the name of the catamaran from *Golden Cockerel* to *Tahiti Bill*, just to prove to any doubters that his entry was no longer sponsored by the Courage brewery, whose symbol then disappeared from the prow.

Bill Howell was the first solo sailor ever to enter for three Observer Singlehandeds in a row, and he was more determined than ever to get among the trophies. I asked him how he rated his chances. 'I think they are very good, but there's an awful lot of luck in this race. But,' and a broad grin creased his chubby bearded face, 'it's about time I won something.'

The other two multihulls entered were not expected to provide much opposition for the ocean greyhounds. *Lady of Fleet* was a beautifully equipped Solaris cruising catamaran, 41 feet in length, that had been entered by Howell's Australian compatriot Murray Sayle. (In fact, Sayle learned a lot about catamaran handling by sailing as Howell's crew in the 1970 Round Britain.) A journalist, Sayle was to make a film about the crossing for the BBC and also report the event for *The Observer's* rival, *The Sunday Times*.

Architeuthis, Gerard Pestey's 55 foot trimaran from France, was not expected to travel westward very quickly, for all her length. She was very much a cruising yacht, last seen in British waters during the 1972 BP Crystal Trophy for multihulls, in which she finished 19th and last on handicap.

So much for the multihull challenge. How many of the 51 monohulled boats would match it? Obviously the one yacht that everyone thought capable of racing away from the multis, and indeed from all the rest of the fleet, in theory at least, was that gigantic schooner *Vendredi 13*, with '68 veteran Jean-Yves Terlain at the helm. Measuring 128 feet overall, she looked to be an enormous handful for any solo sailor. But she had been carefully designed, by the successful American Dick Carter, specifically for singlehanding.

She had a narrow, shallow hull made of a fibreglass foam sandwich – like the Kelsall trimarans of Weld and Beswick. Three equal masts, standing about 75 feet above the deck, each carried a boomed staysail of 930 square feet – and that was the limit of the sailplan.

Hasler's comment on this rig is pithy. 'Desperately inefficient, even to windward, with a quite excessive amount of mast and rigging for her sail area. Boomed staysails are rightly regarded as a poor form of headsail, particularly downwind and in light going, and it is quite wrong to regard the race as being a hard thrash to windward for 3,000 miles. Prevailing winds have a habit of not prevailing. In the 1964 race I ran almost dead before the wind most of the way from Ireland to the Grand Banks. After that I had 1,000 miles of light head winds and calms. Neither of these conditions would have suited *Vendredi 13* one little bit.

'It is also reported that she commonly will not tack, but only wear. If this is true she is putting the clock back at least 600 years and adding considerably to the hazards of Plymouth Sound at the start . . . My guess is that she won't win, and I also *hope* that she won't, because she seems to me to be a fascinating experiment in the wrong direction. The boat that wins this race ought to be a useful all-round performer, as all three previous winners have been.

'If the lumbering giant lumbers fast enough to get to Newport first, then we ought to think a bit harder about the rules before the next race. But a better outcome would be if the sea itself were to prove that lumbering giants don't win.'

A hard judgement, though Hasler typically softens the blow by wishing Terlain good luck and good sailing. It's worth remembering, too, that Gliksman thought before the race that Terlain would be the third Frenchman (with Colas and Vidal) likely to be within the first five.

Vendredi 13 was 80 per cent longer than the next biggest monohull in the entry lists – Gerard Dijkstra's *Second Life*. This was an Ocean 71 class boat, sister ship to *Ocean Spirit*, which Robin Knox-Johnston and Leslie Williams had sailed to victory in the 1970 Round Britain race. They had found the big ketch a massive commitment with a crew of two, but it must also be said that they had started the race with the boat far from properly prepared.

Could Dijkstra, a 27 year old yacht sails and fittings designer from Amsterdam, really control such a large vessel in Atlantic conditions and handle her huge sails efficiently? There was some doubt, but the experts were keeping in mind that the young Dutchman had incorporated many of his own design ideas into the deck gear. If they worked, the boat could be very fast indeed.

Perhaps a surer bet among the monohulls was the long and slim *Strongbow*, entered by another veteran of the 1968 race, Martin Minter-Kemp. He had succeeded where so many others had failed, in getting commercial sponsorship for his boat. Bulmers, who make the cider called Strongbow, put up the cash for this unusual design by Michael Pipe – a 65 foot long big sister to the experimental *Slithy Tove*, which had been so impressive in the 1970 Round Britain. A mere 10 feet in the beam, she quickly proved on her trials that Pipe's theories provide fast boats in the right conditions, pushing the speedo round to 20 knots and then some.

But how often would conditions be right during the crossing to Newport? Again, the coldly analytical comment of Hasler is worth recording. 'She is, in effect, a giant canoe, relatively far narrower even than *Vendredi 13*. And we just don't know how well such an extreme hull can keep going. She will fly along when the conditions are right, but how will she average?'

Next biggest on the list among the monohulls was Joël Charpentier's schooner *Wild Rocket* (63 feet overall). But the Frenchman was not expected to be among the leaders for long, since, like Pestey's trimaran, his yacht was designed mainly for cruising.

But the pair of boats that came next in size were not to be taken lightly by any of the competitors. They were *British Steel* and *Gipsy Moth V*, both from the board of Robert Clark.

Chay Blyth's *British Steel*, the boat in which he sailed around the world nonstop from east to west, was loaned to yet another of the singlehanders who had proved themselves in the 1968 race – bank manager Brian Cooke. This was an instance where neither boat nor crew were required by the Royal Western to provide evidence of a 500 mile qualifying cruise – the boat had certainly proved its capacity for solo passage-making, and Cooke's fine performance in getting *Opus* to Newport in sixth fastest time four years before was evidence enough of his ability.

British Steel was, of course, mainly designed for going to windward, whereas Sir Francis Chichester's *Gipsy Moth V*, just 2 feet shorter at 57 feet overall, had evolved principally as a downwind boat, in which the most famous singlehander of all had attempted to cross 4,000 miles of the Atlantic at the incredible pace of 200 miles a day. He missed that target by just over two days, but he did complete 1,000 miles in one five-day sprint – a valiant feat for a man nearing his seventieth birthday. Now here he was taking up the challenge once again, even though his three score years and ten had been completed.

There were some who thought he would never get started, for illness had troubled him a lot since he returned from the transatlantic dash. But I knew he would be there at the helm of *Gipsy Moth V* on the day of the start if it were humanly possible, for I remembered the look in his eyes when we talked about the possibility of his going for the Observer race more than a year earlier, on the night he returned to the Royal Western after taking *Gipsy Moth V* more than 18,000 miles around the North Atlantic.

The verdigris on the hinges of his spectacles glittered and the eyes twinkled with humour as he said to me, 'Well, you know, I like a bit of sport.'

There were two other yachts entered which measured more than 50 feet – and with such a fleet of greyhounds, it seemed one had to have at least that measurement to stand any chance of being the outright winner – Jim Ferris's *Whisper* is a Morgan 54 from the board of Charlie Morgan. Ferris brought her across the Atlantic for the start in 24 days, so there could be little doubt about her ability to move fast through the water.

The second was the latecomer Franco Faggioni, with his 50·7 foot cutter *Sagittario*.

Faggioni caused something of a stir with his entry, for it arrived well after the 17 April deadline. At first the Royal Western Yacht Club refused it, but then the Chief of Staff of the Italian Navy, Admiral Roselli Lorenzini, pleaded the case of Captain Faggioni, who was to be sponsored by the Italian Navy. Admiral Lorenzini approached the British First Sea Lord, Admiral Sir Michael Pollock, who in turn wrote to Captain Terence Shaw in Plymouth. 'The Italian public had already been told that the yacht was entered,' said Admiral Carrado Vittori, the Italian naval attaché in Britain. 'Our navy set much store by the entry.'

So the Royal Western relented and allowed Faggioni's entry to go on the list, with an 18 hour penalty. Captain Shaw explained, 'I don't like it, but I think it's right.' It was at this time that the organising club also added Gerard Curvelier's name (with a 17 hour penalty).

But if the rest of the fleet had little chance of being first into Newport, they still had a good chance of going hard for two other prizes – the monohull handicap and the new trophy for boats up to 35 feet in length. As the entries came in, it became clear that there would be hot competition for the second

of these two. Perhaps the favourite in this section was Alain Gliksman, with his sleek little sloop *Toucan* (34·5 feet). Some people thought he had chosen this boat in preference to *Raph*, the 58 foot ketch that had been well up with the leaders in the 1968 race until rudder trouble forced her retirement, because he wanted the French to sweep the board. He could leave the outright prize to Terlain and Colas, they surmised, while he concentrated on the up to 35 foot section.

But I don't believe this for a moment. I spoke to Gliksman at the pre-race party in *The Observer*'s London office and he told me then that he really had no option about which boat to choose. *Raph* belongs to a building firm which was not interested in sponsoring an Observer race effort in 1972, so he had fallen back on the smaller craft. 'It has a very good ballast ratio and is very fast,' he said. 'Of course it doesn't go at 15 or 20 knots like some other competitors, but considering that the winner's average speed has always been about six or seven knots I'm happy to think this boat can do that sort of speed most of the time. I have beaten many Class I boats in her.'

One of Gliksman's challengers in the class up to 35 feet was another '68 contender – Claus Hehner from West Germany. He was again entering *Mex*, the 35 foot sloop in which he finished 14th four years earlier, in the slowish time of 41½ days. Of Gliksman's compatriots going for the same trophy, two were attractive girls. Marie-Claude Fauroux would be at the helm of *Aloa VII*, a class boat entered by the makers, SEB Marine of France (they also supplied *Aloa I* for Marie-Claude's compatriot, Yves Olivaux); while Anne Michaelof would sail a 30·6 foot sloop called, somewhat enigmatically, *P.S.* The original name of the yacht, which was sponsored by a cigarette company in Holland, was *Pieter Stuyvesant*, but the Royal Western had invoked the new sponsorship ruling against that, even though there was some talk of the boat commemorating the first mayor of New York, whose tercentenary fell in 1972!

There were another nine boats measuring between 30 and 35 feet, making 14 in all, so it seemed certain that the new trophy would be hard fought for. And it was an international field too, for it included Jerry Cartwright from America in his 32·4 foot cutter *Scuffler III*; Wolf Kirchner from West

Germany, in the 32·3 foot sloop *White Dolphin*; Hubert Bargholtz, from Sweden, with his 32·2 foot sloop *White Lady*, and Edoardo Guzzetti, from Italy, in a 32·6 foot sloop called *Namar IV*.

Against them, from Britain, came Harry Mitchell, a car mechanic from Southsea, with his far from young 33 foot sloop *Tuloa*; Chris Elliott and John Holtom in their Northney 34s *Lauric* and *La Bamba of Mersea*; Martin Wills in his 31 foot sloop *Casper*, and the rugged Marine Commando captain Mike McMullen with his Contessa 32 called *Binkie II*. They were all tough and experienced seamen who would give the overseas competitors a good fight. The new trophy looked set for a thrilling first contention.

For those boats of less than 30 feet, as in previous races, the main object of the exercise was simply to get to the other side. And it was gratifying to see how many solo sailors there were who were keen enough to go in this somewhat unrewarding section of the fleet – not all from Britain. Richard Konkolski of Czechoslovakia brought his 22·5 foot yawl *Niké* from the Baltic to Plymouth for the race; Heiko Krieger of West Germany entered his 29·2 foot sloop *Tinie* (appropriately named in this company); Robert Lancy Burn brought his 28 foot sloop *Blue Gipsy* from South Carolina; and Frenchman Gerard Curvelier just scraped into the lists, albeit with a 17 hour penalty for late qualification, with his 21 foot sloop *Tang'O*.

Their British rivals included some of the most interesting entries, even though they might be among the smallest boats in the fleet. For example, dear old *Jester* was back again, once more with Michael Richey at the helm – the only yacht to have taken part in every Observer Singlehanded. This time Richey had determined to take a quicker route than the trade winds course which made him so slow in 1968.

There was also *Blue Smoke*, a stock Kingfisher 26 for naval lieutenant Guy Hornett to sail (as a distinct change from watch-keeping over nuclear engines in a Polaris submarine). *Blue Smoke* is a twin-keeler, the first ever to enter for an Observer race. Blondie Hasler's comment is again pertinent. 'Twin-keeled monohulls are popularly supposed not to sail well. I believe this is only true of twin-keelers that have been poorly designed – and I hope *Blue Smoke*'s performance will prove it.'

And the British contingent also included the smallest yacht ever to have been accepted for an Observer Singlehanded – the 19 foot Hunter class cruiser *Willing Griffin*, which had been entered by a 28 year old actor, David Blagden. Though she was a stock boat, *Willing Griffin* had been specially prepared and modified for the Atlantic passage. Fast for her length, she was obviously going to make considerable demands on the stamina of her skipper. Indeed, while on his qualifying cruise, Blagden had been forced to signal for assistance because a fierce easterly had knocked the boat down three times and sapped all his energy. Not the best augury for the race, perhaps, but Blagden himself seemed quite unperturbed by the experience.

Rounding off this small-boat class were Eric Sumner's Folkboat *Francette* – that first lonely entry a year before the start and so rejoicing in the sail number 1, Richard Clifford's Contessa 26 *Shamaal*, Andrew Spedding's 28 foot sloop *Summersong*, and a pair of Listang class sloops at 24·8 foot overall. They were Max Barton's *Bristol Fashion* and Bob Salmon's *Justa Listang*.

Though not the most prepossessing entries, they still provided some interesting snippets of information for the enthusiasts following the build-up to the 1972 race. Richard Clifford, for example, is a Royal Marines lieutenant who specialises in amphibious operations. Just five weeks before the start of the race he found himself in mid-Atlantic rather earlier than he expected, when he parachuted from an RAF Hercules to the aid of the ocean liner QE2. An anonymous telephone caller in the United States had told Cunard that there were bombs aboard the liner which would be detonated unless a certain amount of cash was paid over. Clifford and three other bomb disposal experts dropped to the liner in order to make a search and, if possible, dispose of any bombs that might exist. They found nothing.

Bob Salmon's entry in *Justa Listang* also had its intriguing background story. Salmon is a professional photographer who lives close to Plymouth and spends most of his working life there. In 1968, *The Observer*'s picture desk commissioned him to get pictures of all the competitors for that year's Singlehanded. Moving around Millbay Dock and talking to the singlehanders, he suddenly caught the infectious enthusiasm that makes a man take on the Atlantic alone in a small boat. Between 1968 and

1972 he did more and more sailing, then bought *Justa Listang* and determined to complete the qualifying cruise. But bad weather kept him and his small boat pinned in Plymouth until the last moment. He then sailed out into the Atlantic, completed just 502 miles and returned to Plymouth on the day entries closed, putting his formal application on the Sailing Secretary's desk a mere three hours before the midnight deadline on 17 April.

There remain another 15 yachts to account for – the monohulls that are too big for the up to 35 foot trophy and less than the 50 foot that would make them contenders for the outright prize. Their entrants had perhaps only one aim, apart from merely getting safely to the other side of the Atlantic – the handicap trophy for monohulls. Of the 15, six were British and four French, though the French attack was reduced to four when *Myth of Malham*, the fine old ocean racer that Noel Bevan had sailed into 8th place four years earlier, sprang a leak and had to be abandoned off the French coast some weeks before the start. It meant that Frenchman Jean-Pierre Levaire was the first to disappear from the final entry list, though far from being the first tragedy of the race and its build-up.

The remaining French contenders in this group were Marc Linski's *Isles du Frioul*, a 47·9 foot sloop; the 42·8 foot stainless steel hulled sloop *Onyx* of Eugene Riguidel, and Pierre Chassin's 44·3 foot sloop *Concorde*. Their running mate was the Swiss Guy Piazzini, with his 45·5 foot ketch *Cambronne*. Though born in Switzerland and proudly flying the Swiss flag, he lives in France and was closely associated with the French entries.

Their British rivals were a very mixed bunch. Most notable was Peter Crowther's 64-year-old gaff cutter *Golden Vanity*. Measuring 38 feet, she was launched in Dartmouth in 1908 as a floating home-cum-studio for a marine artist. 'She's an amazing boat,' Crowther told me, 'with no self-steering gear. I have a line from the staysail around the wheel on a shot cord and she sails herself perfectly. I think I could average about 100 miles a day. But I need some wind – if it's all westerlies we'll spend years doing it. But with a good wind and a nice big sea – because she's very heavy – we'll just pounce along.'

Another boat that promised to be easy to spot in the mêlèe at Plymouth was *Ròn Glas*, the Chinese lugsail-rigged schooner entered by Jock McLeod.

With a hull designed by Angus Primrose and measuring 47 feet overall, this yacht was claimed to be fast as well as easy to sail. McLeod used to be Blondie Hasler's partner and thus shares his enthusiasm for the westernised Chinese rig. Hasler's comment on this boat betrays his affinities. 'She is believed to be the first seagoing boat in the world whose complete rig can be wholly handled from inside the wheelhouse, where all running ropes are to be found neatly cleated, with their spare ends reeled up nearby. If there were a prize for the most comfortable ride McLeod ought to win it hands down, and I hope he will take along enough occupational therapy to keep himself busy.'

Another schooner, though of conventional rig, was entered in this group by Bruce Webb. Her name is *Gazelle* and she measures 47·5 feet overall. Smaller but likely to be just as fast were Jock Brazier's 46 foot ketch *Flying Angel*, Pat Chilton's 38 foot sloop *Mary Kate of Arun*, and Bob Miller's race-bred 43 foot sloop *Mersea Pearl*.

Miller is an interesting example of how the ambition to do the Observer Singlehanded race can get a grip on a weekend sailor until he becomes almost obsessed by it. Five years ago Bob Miller and the Millermen had become such a popular band in Britain that the leader was experiencing a very hectic life and thinking it was about time he found some relaxation from the constant pressure of one-night stands and recording sessions. So he decided to return to his boyhood love of sailing. He bought a small cruising yacht, moved his home to West Mersea on the Essex coast, and started to enjoy his occasional days off.

Then he began making longer passages, found he enjoyed the thrill of getting where he intended to, despite tide, winds, currents, and shoals, and in no time his mind began to turn to the transatlantic passage. For the 1972 race he sold his class cruiser and bought the Dick Carter designed *Mersea Pearl*. This fast sloop had started life as *Rabbit II*, when it won its class in the 1967 Fastnet Race, and was later sailed by such well known figures in British offshore racing as Ron Amey and David Powell.

'She's a beautiful boat to look at,' Miller told me, 'and very fast. I've sunk myself in debt to get her.'

That leaves five boats in this 35 to 50 foot group to be accounted for. They are the yachts of two Poles, two Italians, and a Belgian. Teresa Remiszewska was the first woman to enter for the 1972 race. She is a highly qualified sailor from Gdynia – something of a pioneer among women sailors in her country, in fact. Her yacht, the 42 foot yawl *Komodor*, was sponsored by the Polish Navy. Also from Gdynia came the entry of Zbigniew Puchalski, a 37 year old sailing champion who retrieved his 38·8 foot sloop *Miranda* from the bottom after she had sunk and completely rebuilt her. He visited Britain in *Miranda* in September of 1971 after a 2,000 mile solo cruise in the Atlantic, and told Joanna Kilmartin how hard he had worked to get the boat fit to face the ocean. 'My very nice, very old *Miranda* has not big chance in race,' he said. 'Next time I change boat. If there is little wind and no storm I have chance because she is very fast. Like a beautiful womans you marry, I know all her defects and I love her all the same.'

The sole Belgian in the entry list was Oscar Debra with his 46 foot ketch *Olva II*. He was expected to finish somewhere near the one Italian in this group, Ambrogio Fogar, with his 38·2 foot sloop *Surprise*.

And that completed the total of 59 competitors. *Myth of Malham*'s sad end quickly brought that down to 58, but it was far from being the only tragedy of the early stages. Commander Bill King had to withdraw his entry back in February because his junk-rigged schooner *Galway Blazer* had been, as he put it, 'torpedoed by a killer whale' 200 miles off the southeast corner of Western Australia when she was being sailed back to Britain for the race.

Commander King managed to patch the gaping hole in the boat's side and struggle back to Perth, but there was no hope of getting her repaired in time to compete.

An earlier disaster struck the character of the 1968 race, Frenchman Joan de Kat. Hugely impressed by Tom Follett's fast time in *Cheers*, de Kat had built a 53 foot steel proa which he called *Yo-Yang*. In May of 1971 he set out for the Caribbean, partly as a trial run and partly to recoup the expenses of building the boat by charter work. Sailing off Finisterre, the outrigger hull began to work loose and de Kat and his crew had to take to the rubber dinghies. They were picked up and returned to port by a cargo boat, but when they went back to salvage the proa she had gone.

Another proa failed to make the starting list. She was *Tai-Tai*, the revolutionary design of Michael Bond, which came to grief during his qualifying cruise in the North Sea in March 1972. Again the two hulls began to part and the boat had to be abandoned. Bond was rescued by a Danish ship and taken to Copenhagen.

There was talk of another proa, a 55 footer, that never got into the lists, and even of a 52 foot hydrofoil which scarcely got past the vague rumour stage. Anthony Churchill, the yachting journalist who navigates aboard Prime Minister Edward Heath's offshore racer *Morning Cloud*, hoped to have a 103 foot three-masted schooner called *Sundancer* as his entry (she was designed and built long before *Vendredi 13*), but insurance and maintenance problems prevented her being properly prepared before the qualifying deadline.

Perhaps the saddest tragedy of all was the experience of Bill Gubbins, whose 39 foot *Sea Jade 72* was wrecked off the south coast near Worthing, during April 1972. In gale-force winds the boat's mast stay snapped and the owner lost control. He fired rescue flares and then had to swim to safety when the craft hit a sandbank. A lifeboat was launched but the yacht was too close inshore to be reached with safety, though the local yacht club claimed later that its specialist teams, trained for exactly this kind of rescue, were available close by if only somebody had called them.

But the build-up to every Observer Singlehanded race has its hard luck stories. As May turned into June and the huge fleet for the 1972 race began to gather in Plymouth, it was time to forget about the past, for 58 boats and solo sailors were on the threshold of a great new adventure. Their thoughts were totally occupied with the future.

8   Plymouth preliminaries

With *Myth of Malham* no longer in the running, 58 yachts were expected in Millbay Dock by the evening tide of Monday, 12 June. That was the deadline set by the Royal Western to allow sufficient time for the various race committees to do their scrutineering before giving each boat its inspection certificate and clearance to start the race.

Only 48 yachts made that deadline. Of the ten boats that missed it, three were withdrawals and seven late arrivals in Plymouth. The withdrawals included a couple of rather sad stories. John Beswick's *Leen Valley Venturer* was on its way towards Plymouth with plenty of time in hand when it collided with an unidentified coaster in the Bristol Channel. The result was four feet sliced off the bow of the trimaran and the end of Beswick's hopes of getting to Newport. 'I was holding my proper course to the vessel approaching,' he said, 'but he wasn't keeping a proper lookout and didn't alter course or stop. Had I been in a monohull I would have sunk like a stone.'

Bad luck blended with an over-optimistic time schedule put out Hubert Bargholtz, the only Swede to have entered. He set out for Plymouth in *White Lady* from the Canaries, but ran into freak headwinds and had to put back again. By then he had no hope of making the start so he sent his regrets.

Christopher Elliott's temporary exit was in no way attributable to bad management. At the pre-race party in *The Observer* office early in May he looked splendidly fit. A month later a telegram explained that he had been taken into hospital in Portsmouth for an urgent operation, and so had to withdraw. He recovered quickly enough for his entry to be reinstated and he actually sailed from Plymouth on 4 July. That left 55 contenders, of which 54 eventually gathered in Millbay Dock. The lone absentee was Gerard Curvelier, who simply did not appear with his little sloop *Tang'O*. It may be that he thought a 17-hour penalty for late completion of his qualifying cruise was too much of a hurdle to overcome in such a small craft.

The rules required all boats to be in the Millbay inner basin by the Monday five days before the start,

and the drama that previous weekend was not so much about those boats which eventually missed the deadline as about the one which did make it, even if at the last possible moment. For anxious telephone calls to *The Observer* London office from Paris indicated that Jean-Yves Terlain's backers were worried about whether he could get to Plymouth in time. We had heard that a lot of last-minute work was being done on the boat in St Nazaire – maybe that had caused the delay.

In the driving rain and heavy mist which welcomed the sailors to Plymouth that day it was virtually impossible to get a sighting of the huge schooner from the usual vantage points. So when she did eventually loom up out of the mist her arrival was all the more dramatic. Suddenly the questions everybody had been asking seemed to have a new significance. Looking along that deck which seemed to go on for ever, glancing up at those three massive masts, it seemed impossible to believe that one man could remain master of such a machine across 3,000 miles of turbulent ocean.

The late arrivals included two of the three women competitors. Teresa Remiszewska was finding it harder to get down the Channel than she anticipated, and eventually made Plymouth two days late on the Wednesday. Anne Michailof steered her *P.S.* into the dock the previous afternoon, with the words Pieter Stuyvesant still looming large along her bows. 'She's got some painting to do tomorrow,' said a member of the committee. Madame Michailof had been delayed in France by a series of wildcat strikes which prevented some of her stores and equipment arriving to schedule. Shades of those last-minute alarums in 1968.

Gerard Pestey's big trimaran *Architeuthis* glided into the dock on Tuesday morning. He was shattered to hear that he had earned a penalty, for he had been off the Eddystone light the night before but decided not to come in because the visibility was so bad and he had no engine in his boat, so it seemed safer to wait. The two Germans, Wolf Kirchner with *White Dolphin* and Claus Hehner with *Mex*, also had problems making their way down from Dover and got in two days late. And the same applied to the quiet Belgian, Oscar Debra, with his *Olva II*.

Now they were all met. By Tuesday afternoon the rain passed over and the sun began to shine. All round Millbay Dock hatches were opened, clothes hung out to dry, essential tasks attended to and, most of all, opinions ventilated about who would get to Newport when. Obviously, *Vendredi 13* was the favourite, and it came as no surprise to hear that Ladbrokes had made her well ahead of the field at 5–2 (she shortened from 4–1 after a number of French punters who came over for the Derby at Epsom the previous week had shown their faith in the big schooner – one even putting down £1,000 in the expectation of picking up four times that amount).

But there seemed to be a general unwillingness to believe that 'the monster' would actually complete the course and next best guesses with many of the more knowledgeable around the dockside were the fast trimarans *Pen Duick IV* and *Three Cheers*. Both were obviously well-prepared and raring to go. Alain Colas seemed ruthlessly determined in the best Tabarly tradition. When I suggested that we have a general talk about the boat and his prospects he said, politely but firmly, 'Not now. I will talk to you in Newport. Now I am keyed up for the race and I don't want any distractions.' His boat sat starkly in one corner of the dock, its bare aluminium structure well-weathered now compared with the bright newness of four years before.

The *Three Cheers* crew could hardly have provided a more complete contrast. Tom Follett was being his admirably amiable self, advising the first-timers, chatting to everyone and looking very relaxed. Dick Newick was pleased to show anyone over the new trimaran, which turned out to be surprisingly roomy below, with two bunks set into the flared bridge sections between the hulls. Such a contrast to the minimal accommodation on the 1968 boat *Cheers*, which came sailing up the Sound to greet her younger sister, manned by a crew from the Exeter Maritime Museum, where *Cheers* now rests.

Tom Follett reckoned, in all seriousness, that he could get to Newport in 16 days if he was lucky with the weather – and we all started to rethink our travelling schedules. It would hardly do for the winner to arrive on the other side before anybody was there to greet him!

Over at Mashford's yard at Cremyll were the two big Robert Clark boats, *Gipsy Moth V* and *British Steel*. There had been some concern about the health of Sir Francis Chichester, but though he looked thinner he was obviously drawing strength from the mounting excitement as start day neared. On the Thursday evening he presided happily over the Royal Western's dinner for the competitors in his new capacity as Commodore of the club.

Brian Cooke seemed more tense about the adventure ahead. He caught an inopportune cold and looked below his peak, but he was no doubt heartened to hear that Chay Blyth was putting money on *British Steel* because he thought Cooke 'would drive her harder than I could'. Martin Minter-Kemp had some last-minute problems, too. *Strongbow* looked superb – long and sleek and somehow very fast even when moored – but the rudder stock had become bent in some mysterious way, and Minter-Kemp was concerned about whether it might happen again during the race.

Bill Howell's *Tahiti Bill* was proudly displaying her new name, while the skipper was welcoming everyone aboard with his habitual bonhomie. His Australian compatriot Murry Sayle was also making lots of friends quickly, while the builders of *Lady of Fleet* seemed to be making the most of the opportunity to display their wares to an interested crowd, for two more Solaris catamarans came into the dock during the week. In the same way the French makers of the Aloas which Marie-Claude Fauroux and Yves Olivaux were to sail sent over *Aloa III* to sit between them and act as tender.

In contrast to all the hustle and bustle in some camps were a pair of very relaxed sailors. Aboard the marvellous old cutter *Golden Vanity*, Peter Crowther pottered happily among a jumble of ropes, pipes, odds and ends. He was splicing a rope when I walked by and he called cheerfully 'The sun is shining so I'm just doing a few odd jobs. But I've got to leave something to panic about on Friday.' Beside him on the deck stood a bicycle. An inquisitive lady asked him what it was for. 'To get around the ship with,' he replied with a smile.

Not all was sweetness and light. At the Thursday briefing session there was some mutterings of 'unseamanlike behaviour' when Alain Colas asked if he could leave his anchor behind on a buoy when the race started Saturday noon. And Jean-Yves Terlain seemed to feel the rest of the competitors were against him just because he had a much bigger boat than any of them.

Particularly upset were the late arrivals. They had no relish for leaving after the rest of the fleet had gone and eventually Oscar Debra announced that he intended to sail on Saturday with the others no matter what anybody said. The Royal Western Race Committee were put in a difficult position: should they disqualify him? The first impulse was yes; then they decided that if the late boats could be inspected and cleared in time they could start with the rest of the fleet on Saturday, but carrying a 24-hour penalty. Otherwise, they could go when they like on Sunday.

The next controversy centred around the handicaps. When the figures were announced on Thursday, there were some cries of delight and some of inconsolable dismay. Joel Charpentier, skipper of the 63-foot schooner *Wild Rocket*, thought his position of sixth fastest in the handicappers' ratings was very hard indeed, and Gerard Pestey was also unhappy, for he was tenth on the list behind *Vendredi 13*, which the committee had obviously made the scratch yacht.

In fact, it was fascinating to see how the handicappers' estimation of what boats should be fastest to Newport varied from the bookmakers' call-over. The Yacht Club list of favourites read *Vendredi 13*, *Pen Duick IV*, *Strongbow*, and *Second Life*, a first four that few would dispute, although Ladbrokes made *Three Cheers* third favourite at 6–1. But after that the lists varied considerably.

British Steel came fifth in the bookmaker's list, but eighth in the eyes of the handicappers. They also rated *Wild Rocket* and *Architeuthis* as likely to be sixth and tenth fastest, whereas Ladbrokes put both boats among the 20–1 rest of the field shots. But the biggest surprise was that the committe rated *Cap 33* fast enough to be fifth in the list, ahead of *Three Cheers*, *British Steel*, *Gipsy Moth V*, and *Trumpeter*.

At the other end of the scale, some boats seemed to have very generous allowances over the scratch yacht. David Blagden was delighted with his figure – he could take 41½ days more than *Vendredi 13* and still beat her on handicap. Similarly Jock McLeod was very happy with his 22½-day allowance – it meant that his 47-footer *Ròn Glas* was reckoned to be on a par with Anne Michailof's 30-foot *P.S.* and a little slower than Mike McMullen's Contessa 32.

There were, of course, some protests, and a few figures were reconsidered. Chief sufferer was Blagden, whose generous margin was reduced to just under 37 days.

As the week went by it was fascinating to walk around the dock and see who was prepared and who was not. Aboard Jean-Marie Vidal's *Cap 33* there was seldom any sign of activity. The slim trimaran was obviously all set to go. On Charpentier's *Wild Rocket*, by contrast, there was frenzied activity all the week by an army of helpers, and when I went below to seek out the French physical education instructor on Friday, the inside of his schooner looked absolutely chaotic, though Charpentier himself was quite cool and unstressed.

The Czech contingent made quite a few friends. Richard Konkolski's handsome bearded face seemed always to wear a big smile, and his little wife Miroslava gained approving glances from the women among the thousands who visited the docks during the week for the wifely way she festooned the rigging with Richard's freshly-washed shirts and underwear. 'My wife is determined that I am going to get off to a clean start,' said Konkolski.

Bob Miller was prevented from getting on with his last-minute preparations by the insistent demands of his public. Having sailed *Mersea Pearl* into Plymouth, he had to dash off on Tuesday to lead the Millermen at a wedding party in the Savoy Hotel, coming back to the boat on the sleeper train. Even on Friday he was still busy, for the Millermen came down to Plymouth and together they played a last gig at HMS *Raleigh* at Torpoint. Through it all the bandleader-mariner remained cheerful and untroubled, though he was slightly perturbed when the technicians could not get his radio to function properly, considering his commitment to report daily to the BBC's Tony Brandon show and to make a weekend call to *The Observer*.

The girl sailors were attracting a lot of attention from the dozens of journalists. Marie-Claude Fauroux told one of them that she was prepared to take any bets that she would be right up there with the tough guys at the finish. The Polish woman sailor Teresa Remiszewska found time to talk to the Press also, although her boat was far from ready. They found it difficult to believe that she admitted to being 43, for she looked far too young to have a son at university.

Her problems were considerable. The battery on

Morning departure. Last-minute activity in Millbay Dock on the morning of 17 June. In the foreground, the two ill-fated Listangs of Bob Salmon (left) and Max Barton.
Photo: Frank Page

The friendly exhortations from Eugene Riguidel's chums turned out to be all in vain – he was the only one of the French faction that did not complete the course to Newport.
Photo: Frank Page

Bob Lancy Burn was making no great claims for the performance of Blue Gipsy as she sat in the still waters of Millbay Dock before the start of the race. Yet the little sloop sailed swiftly enough to take second place in the monohull handicap listings.

Photo: Frank Page

Despite a time penalty for late qualification, Franco Faggioni sailed his 51 foot cutter Sagittario into ninth place in just under twenty-nine days. Like Jim Ferris, he believed in being able to sit comfortably while at the helm.
Photo: Chris Smith

*All smiles now. Carlo Mascheroni looked
cheerful enough when he set off for Newport
from Plymouth, but he soon altered course for
Gibraltar and retired from the race.*
Photo: Frank Page

Bob Salmon made himself conspicuous among the huge starting fleet by the red and white striped genoa on his Listang. Sadly, he was dismasted and never reached Newport.
Photo: Frank Page

Golden Vanity looked old-fashioned but
enormously dignified in the fleet in Plymouth
Sound. She failed to finish within the sixty–
day race period.
Photo: Frank Page

Pierre Chassin had the company of Billy the Alsatian during his transatlantic passage. Billy was raring to go at Plymouth, but by the time Concorde arrived at Newport, the dog was very pleased to be on dry land again.
Photo: Frank Page

Phil Weld looked very pleased with himself as Trumpeter flashed past the press launch in Plymouth Sound, for his trimaran had just tacked inside Vendredi 13. But the advantage was short-lived: Trumpeter found more than her share of holes in the wind during the crossing.
Photo: Frank Page

This shot of the murky scene on the morning of the start shows the three successful French trimarans in close company. Pen Duick IV (sail number 25) lies behind Architeuthis (29), while Cap 33 (33) is off to the left between Mex (38) and Cambronne (56).
Photo: David Newall Smith

Anne Michailof seemed very determined to get to America when she left Plymouth in P.S., but her 30 foot sloop proved rather slow and she was the last of the French sailors to cross the line. Because of her time penalty she was placed last among the forty boats which completed the course within the time limit.

The long and short of it. David Blagden's
19 foot Hunter Willing Griffin *creeps cheeki*
along the side of the 128 foot Vendredi 13 *a*
they prepare to leave Plymouth at the start.
The smaller boat took more than twice as lon
to get to Newport, but it beat the schooner on
handicap.
Photo: Frank Page

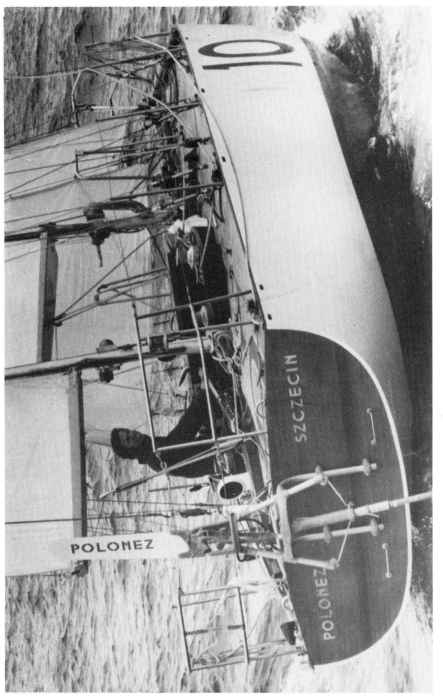

Seen at closer quarters when she was tacking in Plymouth Sound before the start, Chris Baranowski's Polonez turned out to be beautifully constructed in traditional materials – a delight to the eye and fast as well.
Photo: Frank Page

Er . . . excuse me, lady. There is a boat behind you. Marie-Claude Fauroux's Aloa VII is overshadowed by the massive masts of Joel Charpentier's schooner Wild Rocket just before the start at Plymouth.

Headed for third place, Jean-Marie Vidal waves cheerily from Cap 33 to The Observer's circling aircraft eight hours after the start. The trimaran was then well down the field, but Vidal made up a lot of time after passing the Azores.
Photo: Chris Smith

Though he looked well prepared, as Gipsy Moth V passed the press launch just before the start of the race there was continuing concern about Sir Francis Chichester's apparent lack of energy.
Photo: Frank Page

Komodor was flat and seawater was mysteriously getting into the fuel oil tank. Below deck, the small cabin was jumble of lifted floorboards and equipment, but her lucky mascot – of all things a decadent, western traditional Teddy Bear – hung wisely from the roof, overseeing all. On the bookshelf was an odd mixture of books in Polish and English, including Robin Knox-Johnston's *A World of My Own* and a translation of Alec Rose's *My Lively Lady*.

Madame Remiszewska said she thought women could make better sailors than men and that she much preferred sailing on the sea to inland waters. 'The sea is alive and huge. Sailing on it is a challenge.' It is her ambition to be the first woman to sail around the world alone.

Anne Michailof, too, was often asked to produce her ready smile for cameras and television interviewers. 'I am in love with the sea,' she told one reporter. 'When I am on land and I see the sea I long to be on it.' She said that she had found some resistance from men at her entering what is normally considered a masculine preserve. But she was certainly not put off by it. 'My advice to any woman who wants to do things like this is to go ahead and do them. Take no notice of the cynical comments of men.'

Despite hints to me that he might have to withdraw at the last moment, Alain Gliksman arrived in Plymouth with the long, slim *Toucan*. But he was not keen to join the impromptu parties going on around the dock and tried to relieve his obvious tension by getting to sleep with the aid of pills after each day's work on the boat.

'I am scared to death by the thought of the trip,' he said, for all his wide experience. 'It's all very well sailing a few hundred miles in the Channel or in the Bay of Biscay, but the Atlantic is a big ocean.' Yet, there was no thought of pulling out. 'I've got to go now,' he said. 'If I didn't I would never know if I am a man or a mouse.' For my money, it takes a real man to talk so frankly, especially at such a time.

Amid the tensions of the build-up week there were a number of felicitous moments which helped to ease the nervous strain. The unexpected arrival of free gifts, for example. A French firm handed out cartons of wine to fortify the solo navigators against the Atlantic, and Wrigley's produced enough chewing gum to keep every set of jaws moving constantly across 3,000 miles of sea.

The Thursday night dinner produced its own ambiance of good fellowship. Jack Odling-Smee raised prolonged applause by announcing a new trophy – for the first woman sailor home. He advised the competitors to be nice to their boats and listen to what they say – an apt warning in view of what happened to Joel Charpentier just 48 hours later. The Chairman of the Race Committee thought that the 1968 record of 19 boats finishing out of 35 starters was bad – he expected a much higher proportion of finishers this year.

Tom Follett spoke at the dinner as well – briefly but wittily. He suggested that all present should contribute to a special fund set up to provide a motor-bike for Jean-Yves Terlain so that he could go forward when necessary!

After the dinner I cornered the tall, rangy American Philip Weld, crew of the Kelsall-designed trimaran *Trumpeter*, and asked him about his theory that the winner would be home in 500 hours. 'You work it out this way,' he said. 'Take 20 days – that's 480 hours – and add 20 to make the round 500. Now you have to sleep around 100 hours, that leaves 400. Take up another 100 for eating and bosuning and you are left with 300 hours you can be at the helm. And it's the time at the helm that makes the difference. This race is going to be won dinghy style.'

Naturally, there were plenty of other competitors planning to drive themselves hard. Bill Howell told me he planned to take a week off his 1968 time of 31½ days. Brian Cooke was planning to take three alarm clocks with him on *British Steel* to make sure that he never slept longer than one hour at a time.

One of the most familiar sights around the Plymouth dockyard during the week was Glin Bennett of Bristol University's Department of Mental Health. He was busily handing out special report cards to most of the English-speaking competitors who had agreed to cooperate in a systematic survey of the problem of fatigue. Most small boat sailors know that after some hours at the helm, when you are cold, wet, tired, hungry, and possibly seasick too, you can easily make errors of judgement which could sometimes be disastrous. Dr Bennett's survey was planned with the intention of finding out what conditions cause this fallibility and, if possible, what advice should be given to small boat sailors about how to avoid it.

Each skipper helping in the scheme was asked to fill in a card each day giving details of his efficiency at navigation and sailing technique, plus some indications of his state of well being. The questions about how each sailor was feeling were cunningly devised – a bar was drawn across the card, and the sailor was simply asked to draw a line across the bar at what seemed the appropriate place between opposite feelings printed at each end of the bar. For example, one pairing was 'ready to drop' and 'full of energy'. It perhaps says something for Dr Bennett's sense of humour that the last item on this list had at one end 'answering these questions is enjoyable' and at the other 'answering these questions is a damned nuisance'.

Somehow, I had the feeling that quite a number of the solo mariners would be making their marks towards the latter end of that line, for in the main they seemed to be an individualistic lot, with the sort of self-containment that does not welcome this kind of probing. After all, the evidence of individualism was all around in Millbay Dock. Just look at *Golden Vanity*, for example. What could be more of a spit in the eye to conventional living than to sail a 64-year-old gaff cutter singlehanded to America? Especially when you take a cat and five kittens for company, as Peter Crowther did.

The neatly-bearded Frenchman Pierre Chassin had animal company, too. He wrote to the Royal Western and asked if he could bring a dog. Mindful of Britain's quarantine laws, the club returned a definite negative. So M. Chassin brought the dog, kept it aboard during the week before the race and only allowed it above deck while he was manoeuvring for the start. It barked away joyfully, seeming to relish the idea of a sail to the New World.

There were, of course, last-minute alarms. Some of the French competitors were hard-pressed to find the radio signal beacons which they were required to carry according to the rules of the race. When they protested that such things were not authorised by the controlling bodies in France, Captain Terence Shaw replied firmly that Alain Colas had written to the Royal Western in plenty of time and found out how to get a beacon. If he could do it, so could the others. And of course, they did.

The American Jim Ferris burnt some late-night oil on his self-steering gear. He had completed his qualifying cruise without the gear and was carefully putting it together during the week in Millbay. The finishing touches were made at 8.30 on Saturday morning, just as the naval launches came chugging into the dock to tow the yachts out to the start line.

But it will always be thus. Most of these sailors knew they would be entering for the Observer Singlehanded two or three years before. Each of them had completed a 500-mile qualifying cruise at least two months in advance. Every yacht had been in Plymouth for best part of a week before the start. And even so, there were dozens of unfinished jobs.

Eventually, the time came to call a halt. What was still undone would have to stay undone. The critical moment of the big adventure had arrived. The day which had been ringed on hundreds of calendars around the world had dawned. It was Saturday, 17 June. And this was the start.

9 The Start

That Saturday morning dawned grey and still. Thousands of heads must have turned to the early morning sky and wondered if we were in for a repeat of the 1968 start – when the Reverend Stephen Pakenham wrote himself into sailing history by rowing his ketch *Rob Roy* across the Sound because there was absolutely no wind at all.

But the wind was merely sleeping. As the sun climbed behind the shrouding clouds so the breeze piped up and by the time the 52 yachts which started that day were ready to cross the line there was a steady blow of force 4 to 5 from sou'-sou'-west. By the time I went down to Millbay for a last stroll around the dock just after eight o'clock the burgees were already stirring at the mastheads and the smell of bacon and egg breakfasts was carried across the water on the freshening breeze.

There was an air of almost forced calm among many competitors. With four hours to go until the start it seemed silly to be getting too tense. But in fact there was only 30 minutes to go before the dock gates opened and the towing boats would arrive to take the yachts out to the start area. Some sailors remained below deck, doing last-minute sorting of stores; some were saying their farewells to friends and helpers; some – like Jim Ferris – were still working hard on vital equipment.

Martin Wills pushed past me on the dockside, looking more resentful than anxious. 'I still haven't got my water,' he said. 'I've been on at them about it all week,' and disappeared muttering. The French contingent had obviously made light of the last night in port. Eugene Riguidel's rigging carried a hand-painted streamer reading 'Allez Onyx. Good luck Eugene'. And one of the French tender craft had been made a kind of unofficial entry, with aerosol shaving soap used to inscribe a sail number on the forehatch. The number? What else but 69?

Alongside Eric Sumner's *Francette* lay the Training Ship *Larvik*, the Sea Cadet boat on which Eric had served for several trips in his capacity as a Lieutenant-Commander of the Corps and sail training officer for the north-west area. Anne Michailof's yacht had its name abbreviated, but with sticky tape rather than paint, and one had the feeling that it could soon be stripped off with continual dipping into heavy seas.

Bob Miller drove into the dock in a taxi. Sailing friends from West Mersea had laid on a good luck party for him on the last night in port. It may not have been the wisest thing to do but Bob had obviously enjoyed it – he was smiling broadly as he climbed down to the deck of *Mersea Pearl*.

And just in time, for soon the naval power craft were streaming through the opened dock gates and the armada of boats began to move out towards the start area. By the time *Vendredi 13* was moving majestically out there was a sizeable crowd on the dock, the clouds had thinned and the wretched British summer of '72 seemed to have relented enough to provide a gilding of sunlight on the early morning scene.

The crowd would have liked to see *Gipsy Moth V* and Sir Francis Chichester, but they were over at Cremyll still, waiting to be towed out by one of Mashford's launches. There had been much talk of Sir Francis and his illness during the last days in Plymouth. Many of his close friends were very worried about him, especially since they had heard that he had consulted nine doctors before the race and was advised not to take part.

The trouble seemed to be an alarming lack of red corpuscles in his blood. On the Tuesday morning before the start he could only just struggle out of his bunk on *Gipsy Moth*. He said afterwards that he felt 'as if the marrow had gone wrong'. But later in the week he seemed to feel better, though he looked thin and drawn at the Thursday briefing.

Not surprisingly, he was the centre of much of the journalists' attentions. J R L Anderson, an old friend of Sir Francis, had joined forces with *The Sunday Times* temporarily in order to take Chichester's messages from mid-ocean. He wrote in that newspaper: 'His latest illness appears to derive from some affection of the bone marrow, also affecting the proportion of red corpuscles in the blood. He has had treatment for this including transfusions to restore the proper balance in the blood. He thought he was fit to go.'

Giles Chichester, too, was quoted in the Press about his father. 'I don't know that any doctor advised him not to go. But I don't think he'd go out there with a death wish. As far as we know he is getting over his illness. It's an infection, not leukaemia. He has had bouts of very serious illnesses in the last year.'

Should he have gone at all? Who is to say? As the competing yachts began to fill up the area of Plymouth Sound specially cleared for the race those of us on the Press launch could see Sir Francis sitting apparently quite unconcerned at the helm – alone again at last. But would it be the last time?

By now the Sound was filling rapidly. Royal Navy launches kept small spectator craft out of the way, and the 52 competing boats had plenty of room to manoeuvre as they tacked back and forth, getting the sheets running freely, easing the creases out of the sails. There were 52 yachts because two single-handers who could have gone that morning decided to wait over and leave on the Sunday. They were Wolf Kirchner in *White Dolphin* and Teresa Remiszewska in *Komodor*.

Kirchner reckoned that as he had a 24-hour penalty anyway he might just as well start the next day and have the advantage of about three hours extra tide. Madame Remiszewska was still feeling tired after her hard fight down the Channel and there were some things still to be done to the boat, so she elected to stay in Plymouth one more night.

But now, at last, the minutes were ticking away to noon and the starting gun. Yachts which had anchored calmly in the Sound – *Golden Vanity* and *Jester* had sat quietly together waiting the off while the others sailed past – now weighed their anchors and prepared to move up to the line. We watched amazed the stately progress of *Vendredi 13*. Jean-Yves Terlain handled the massive schooner with quiet aplomb. Gone now were the multi-coloured jeans and the mauve Indian headband which kept his long mane under some measure of control. Now he wore yellow oilskins and a silver crash helmet. Did he expect the three masts to come crashing down on him? No, it seems that the crash helmet was adopted simply as the most comfortable form of headgear he could find. It keeps out the rain and the wind very effectively. Nevertheless, there had been

sceptics who thought it might need to serve a different purpose, for they looked dubiously at the backstay leading up to the rearward mast and then along the top of the other two and down to the forestay. Sure, they said, it was an impressively thick cable, but it included two insulators, because it also served as a radio aerial – and many a yachtsman has suffered dismasting because of the notorious fallibility of insulators.

Suddenly the whole scene was reminiscent of the start of a dinghy race. Most of the fleet was edging up to the line as if seconds were going to be precious at the other end and the thrashing about at the windward end of the line had to be seen to be believed. At last the gun sounded and there was a great surge forward by every boat. Two of the French entries were so keen to get away that they were over the line at the start.

Marc Linski in *Isles du Frioul* beat the gun by 15 seconds and incurred a penalty of 75 minutes. Marie-Claude Fauroux in *Aloa VII* was close behind but she had only transgressed by ten seconds so her penalty was 50 minutes. Marc Linski made a superb getaway and lead the rush towards the western end of the breakwater, while *Vendredi 13* glided across the line down at the leeward end and soon made her extra length count. Bob Salmon's little *Justa Listang* made a good getaway and the French were well represented with Anne Michailof's *P.S.* as well as Eugene Riguidel's *Onyx*. Then Gliksman's *Toucan* came gliding through, passing the tiny *Willing Griffin* on the way. *British Steel* was well up in the centre of the line, too.

Now the spectator craft could mix with the competitors and a flurry of small boats buzzed round the big schooner. Down to windward I picked out the strange shape of *Sumner*, Blondie Hasler's experimental boat with its inevitable Chinese lugsail. It was soon passed by its near relation *Ron Glas*, for Jock McLeod had his two lugsails drawing well. We heard that morning that Jock's ambition was to sail from Plymouth to Newport without needing to put on oilskins. Now that really would be a step forward towards yachts that are easy and comfortable to sail!

But where were *Pen Duick*, *Three Cheers*, *Tahiti Bill*, and *Gipsy Moth V*? Colas' big trimaran could be seen way back, obviously disdaining the mad mêlée on the start line. Similarly, Sir Francis

Chichester brought *Gipsy Moth V* over the line well behind the pack. Then *Three Cheers* came slicing through the fleet. We heard later that Tom Follett intended originally to go out through the eastern end of the breakwater and head down south to make the most of the outgoing tide down the Channel. But the eastern side of the Sound was so crammed with spectator boats that he thought it wise to tack and follow the rest through the western end.

Once she was on to her port tack *Three Cheers* soon showed her speed. She passed boat after boat and sped out of the Sound hard on the heels of the leaders.

Jean-Yves Terlain kept *Vendredi 13* well down to leeward – to the point where the big staysails were beginning to backwind as the schooner drew in close to the Cornish side of the Sound. When at last she did put about she came round beautifully, easily confounding the critics who thought she would have to wear ship. But she had left it late, and others were going about inside her line and getting ahead of her. Philip Weld swung his trimaran around inside the schooner's course and was soon as much as 200 yards ahead. As he sped past the Press boat he called up cheerily to us 'It's at this time I usually do something stupid.'

As *Trumpeter* went by we could see *Binkie II* being pushed along well by Mike McMullen and Bob Miller following up close with *Mersea Pearl*. There too was Chris Baranowski in *Polonez*, making all 45 feet of his ketch work hard. In fact, as they passed out into the Channel the leaders seemed to be Linski, Riguidel, Terlain, Baranowski, Gliksman, and Weld. But by this time there was a great froth of spectator boats about and the fleet was spreading out so much it was difficult to be sure who was ahead of whom.

One of the expected front runners we did not see at all was Bill Howell and *Tahiti Bill*. We discovered later that he had gone out through the eastern end of the breakwater. His compatriot Murray Sayle also took his time getting away with *Lady of Fleet*. Indeed, the following morning's *Sunday Times* proclaimed almost with pride 'Our man last in Singlehanded start'.

The first real drama of the race came soon after the start – that is if one discounts the many potentially disastrous moments that occurred as the boats were tacking to and fro before the start – but every yacht race has those dramas. Within the first two hours Sir Francis Chichester was seen to be heading *Gipsy Moth V* very close in to Penlee Point just where the tide was tending to carry a boat further in towards real danger. While we held our breath he managed to put the big ketch about, while local knowledgeable boatmen reckoned that he was less than a boat's length from running on to the rocks.

But that wasn't the end of it. It now appeared that what had distracted the 70-year-old's attention from his dangerous position was the totally uncontrolled state of his big jib. It seemed to have gone completely round the forestay, for it was now flapping wildly in the breeze and its sheets were wrapped around the forestay in a tangle. Wearily, Sir Francis looked across to us and made a gesture compounded of despair and disgust. With *Gipsy Moth V* now headed away from the land he made his way slowly and laboriously forward to sort out the mess.

But in his confusion he must have selected the wrong halyard to release, for we suddenly saw the staysail starting to fold while the jib flapped on. Realising his mistake, Sir Francis winched the smaller sail into position again and then started on the jib. It seemed to take an age and by now some of the leaders were over the horizon and something like ten miles ahead.

We had to leave him struggling to right the mess. It was time for the Press boat to return to Plymouth, passing the stately shape of *Golden Vanity* still plugging away out of the Sound as we did so.

But the long day was far from over. Back in port I linked up with *Observer* photographer Chris Smith and we set off by car for the airport at St Mawgan, near Newquay. There we hired a light plane and flew off towards the Lizard and Land's End to see if we could identify the leaders. By now it was past 7 o'clock in the evening and the light was beginning to fade in the overcast sky. But as we looked down on the Cornish countryside it was easy to see that the yachtsmen would not want for wind – the trees were working violently and the long manes of the horses in the fields were strung out by the breeze.

No sooner had we passed over the coast than our pilot was picking up yachts all around us. And there, closest to us, was a yellow trimaran. Had we picked up *Three Cheers* at the first attempt? No, as we went down closer I could make out the pencil slim outriggers of Jean-Marie Vidal's *Cap 33*, skidding along quite quickly but very close in to land.

Now we could identify a string of boats quite close together. We picked out the blue superstructure of Bruce Webb's *Gazelle*, the clean lines of Claus Hehner's *Mex*, the little sloop *Namar IV* of Edoardo Guzzetti, and the bigger ketch of his compatriot Carlo Mascheroni. *Chica Boba* was moving through the water well with no mizzen sail set.

Next we came up to Bob Miller's *Mersea Pearl*, well heeled over and leaving a fine wake behind. Then, as we travelled further down the Channel, we caught up with some of the bigger boats that had already made their length count in the first eight hours of the race. The steel hull of Eugene Riguidel's *Onyx* came into sight next. He had obviously capitalised on that good start. Then there was the late entrant Faggioni in the big cutter *Sagittario*, scudding along very impressively not far behind the second biggest boat in the race – Gerard Dijkstra's *Second Life*.

Another gap and we came to Charpentier's *Wild Rocket*, living up to its name in every way – going like a rocket and looking slightly wild with the amount of sail it was carrying. There was a reef in the mainsail, but the big genoa the Frenchman had hoisted looked decidedly risky in the strong breeze that was now blowing.

At last the real thrill. There was the big three-master ahead, obviously moving very fast indeed. She was not far off Land's End and really slicing through the water in most impressive fashion. The three staysails were drawing beautifully and the long hull was heeled over about 20 degrees as it followed a foaming path through the rising chop of the Channel. We circled *Vendredi* three or four times while Chris Smith took his pictures, and more than once I could see at least 30 feet of her great length lift clear of the water on the crest of a wave before crashing down into the next trough in an explosion of spray. '*Vendredi 13* can stand up to anything the Atlantic can dish out,' her designer, Dick Carter, had said, but I must confess that I began to wonder just how much of that sort of bombardment the long hull really could stand.

We calculated that *Vendredi 13* had averaged nearly 15 knots in the first eight hours, beating into the south-westerly which was now blowing really strongly but right on the nose. In fact, as we circled

the big schooner we saw Terlain put her about three times, for he seemed intent upon keeping her as close in to Mount's Bay as possible to avoid the worst of the choppy water further out.

Perhaps *Wild Rocket* was indeed second at that stage – we could not tell. After all, we had not seen *Pen Duick*, or *Three Cheers* or *British Steel*, which should have been finding these conditions ideal. Second or not, *Wild Rocket*'s challenge did not last long, for soon after we had returned to Plymouth we heard that she had blown out her sails and was heading back to the start point in disarray.

Also heading back after just a few hours in the race was the Belgian Oscar Debra in *Olva II*. The hard going soon after the start found a weakness in his fibre-glass fuel tank and it split, disgorging fuel oil over his food and equipment. He told me the sad story on Sunday morning, standing forlornly at the bar of the Royal Western Yacht Club, now strangely quiet and deserted on the morning after the great exodus.

He had planned to sail *Olva II* in the 1968 race, apparently, and had her built then. But it was the old story – delays cropped up and she just was not ready for the start. So he shelved his plans for $3\frac{1}{2}$ years and then worked for six months solidly on *Olva II* as a 1972 entry.

His was not a commercially sponsored entry, but he had been helped to prepare the boat by a number of friends in Belgium, so he was particularly glum that morning to think his race had lasted such a short time and that he was such a disappointment to all those helpers. 'Ah well,' he said after a while, 'perhaps in 1976.' The first retirement of the 1972 race.

The other topic of conversation in Plymouth that Sunday was the reported brush between Marc Linski in *Isles du Frioul* and Jean-Yves Terlain in *Vendredi 13*. It seems they became involved in a kind of luffing match going down the Channel and the big schooner actually struck the steering gear on *Isles du Frioul*. Eye witnesses said that Linski immediately ran up a protest flag. But, of course, the protest could only be heard and deliberated upon in Newport when both yachtsmen had given their account of the incident.

So what would happen if the favourite romped home first and Linski took days, perhaps weeks, to follow him to America? It was the sort of not-very-pleasant-taste-in-the-mouth situation that everyone had hoped to avoid.

But fortunately there was an exciting distraction to our deliberations on the protest problem – Kirchner was setting out in *White Dolphin*. Gallantly declining the offer of a tow, he hoisted sail inside the dock and cleverly tacked across it so that he could just lay the opening by a whisker. He was then faced with a bitter beat across the Sound into the fierce south-westerly which was now up to force 6 inside the breakwater and nearly gale strength outside. His intention was, we heard, to anchor off the breakwater and hope that the wind would drop a little later in the day.

At 10.30, half an hour after *White Dolphin*'s departure, Teresa Remiszewska's *Komodor* came into sight, under a small storm jib and reefed mizzen. There was a good deal of sympathy for the Polish woman skipper as she manoeuvred edgily across the deserted Sound before us and disappeared into the enveloping mist.

So the 54 starters were under way. Already there was one back in harbour and well over a hundred miles of sea separating the first and last. From now on those of us waiting at home would have to struggle to fit together some sort of vague pattern from isolated radio reports, sightings from ships and aircraft and, unfortunately, the sad news of those who failed in their efforts to get to America.

In previous races this had been difficult enough, but we knew that the 1972 event, with more than 50 runners, and such a small proportion carrying radio transmitting equipment, would be a jig-saw with even bigger gaps than before. That very day, Sunday 18 June, we had our first experience of how difficult it would be to keep track, for the BBC sent a spotter plane out from St Mawgan in the morning. Groping along the expected route in poor visibility, Peter Crampton and his team could not find a probable leader. But they did sight *Three Cheers* going well south of Land's End and Alain Gliksman's *Toucan* actually ahead of the American trimaran. But apart from those two, the other yachts found were from the middle-of-the-field group, not the expected front-runners. Still, it was good to know that the little 26-footer *Blue Smoke* was pushing on bravely, that *Ron Glas*'s lugsails were drawing her steadily through the big seas, and that the colourful old cutter *Golden Vanity* was riding out the rough conditions as though she really enjoyed them.

And then they were gone. Gone into a south-westerly gale that felt as though it could blow on for a month. I left Plymouth with a profound admiration for every one of them and set about completing my plans to move to Newport to see them home.

10   *Ways and Means*

The limits to the variations in latitude available to singlehanders taking part in the Observer Single-handed seemed to have been set, before the 1972 event, by a single boat. In 1960 Blondie Hasler took *Jester* way up north, actually reaching 56 degrees north at one point. Eight years later, with Michael Richey at the helm, *Jester* went as far south as 25 degrees north in search of the trade winds.

But as the 1972 race developed into its first full week it seemed unlikely that any boat would follow either of those two extremes. We knew that several sailors had been vastly impressed by *Cheers'* performance in 1968, and the reports that packs of ice on the northern route were heavier than in any year that records have been kept (since 1900) indicated that few would be eager to wander too far in that direction. So it looked as though there would be a fairly even split between those opting for the great circle and those choosing to go down to the Azores.

In the event, the division came quickly, for the fierce southwesterly blows of the first week made decisions imperative. Alain Colas in *Pen Duick IV*, for example, ended his first day's run well to the north of the Scillies, whereas Jean-Marie Vidal in *Cap 33* was already committed to a steep south-westerly track which was to take him down to the 37th parallel and through the islands in the first ten days.

But the interesting point about the later paths followed by the two groups is that they converge again in mid-ocean and run together through what seems to be the worst of the Gulf Stream. In fact, scarcely any boats followed a true great circle route. I can find two possible explanations for this, both borne out by my talks with the competitors as they arrived at Newport. First, those who chose the northern track kept well south of what might have been a more direct course, because they were not anxious to go where icebergs might be lingering. Second, those who veered south in the first week found that they had a difficult choice to make once they had passed the Azores – either to turn well south and hope to get a good southwesterly that would blow them up the eastern seaboard of America

once they had travelled that far, or to let the winds wash them back north again and risk any possible disadvantage from the Gulf Stream.

Most chose the latter course, and found that the last third of their voyage was dogged by light airs, complete calms, and then fog. It is not without significance that Gerard Pestey in *Architeuthis* made very good time for his craft by keeping to the Azores route for as long as he could, while his countryman Jean-Marie Vidal managed to keep even further south and made some good mileages in early July while others further north were finding little or no wind at all.

Of those starting out to keep north of the Gulf Stream, along the traditional winner's route that lies somewhere between the great circle and the rhumb line, most seemed to come south whenever the winds favoured that direction, no doubt re-membering all those ice alerts. Martin Minter-Kemp in *Strongbow* and Brian Cooke in *British Steel* kept further north than most, but the French leaders *Pen Duick IV* and *Vendredi 13* seemed happy enough to swing down to about 42 degrees north and head straight across the ocean for Newport, Gulf Stream or no.

Unlike the 1968 race, there was no great storm to provide a turning point in the whole event. The nearest thing to it was the sudden gale of 1 July. That was the day Tom Follett thought he was going to make a record mileage and ended up running under bare poles. It was also the day that Gerard Dijkstra lost his mast and Marc Linski had the accident which severely damaged his hand. And finally, it was the day that *Strongbow* suffered her second knockdown.

All the sailors reported a similar pattern of events. The wind was blowing strongly in the early part of the day and seemed to be holding steady at about 30 knots. Then suddenly it whipped up much more fiercely, so that rapid reduction of sail was necessary to avoid a catastrophe.

Yet the whole front was through and away very quickly. Minter-Kemp reported hoisting his genoa early the next morning, while Linski complained that from then until 5 July he had no wind at all.

54

Certainly those in the Gulf Stream area had a miserable first week in July – only down to the south Vidal, Howell, and Pestey were whistling along nicely. Howell's choice of the southern route intrigued me, because I knew he had made a very careful study of Follett's passage four years earlier. When he eventually arrived in Newport he was obviously proud of how this had worked out in practice. As he said to Jack Odling-Smee, 'Those of us who have done it before are learning all the time. It's a marvellous race.'

As we shall see later, some of the old hands would have liked the 1968 conditions all over again, storms and all. People like Brian Cooke, Jean-Yves Terlain, and Tom Follett would have relished some really strong blows to scoot along their powerful yachts. But what they got instead were calms and fogs, and days when the wind would pick up suddenly and just as quickly die away again.

On the other hand Alain Gliksman, with his fast but lightly built *Toucan*, would have taken the northern route if he could have foreseen that the weather would be so kind, for then he could have made his little lake sailer skim along even better.

But who can foretell the weather, no matter what electronic aids and weather forecasts are consulted? I was particularly interested to hear the comments of Bill Howell on this topic after the race. He said, 'I decided not to go to the weather briefing and not to listen to any of the weather forecasts. And I missed nothing, for they were all so wrong it was just a joke. If you had taken them seriously you would have found yourself dictating your actions according to what you thought might happen instead of what you could actually see was going on around you.'

He has a point. For instance, the experts reckoned that there would be northwest winds for the start on 17 June, and in fact they turned out to be southwesterlies. In the same way Howell was somewhat sceptical of what the experts reckoned were the limits of the Gulf Stream. They were saying that the lower limit of the adverse current came at about 41 degrees north. Howell contends that in fact the effects could be felt quite strongly at that latitude, which could well have influenced the performance of *Three Cheers*. 'Tom went much further north than I did,' he told me. 'And I reckon he probably lost a day and a half as a result. I kept down around

38 to 39 degrees north and checked whether I was getting any adverse current running against me by comparing my logged mileage against my dead reckoning. In fact, I think I was getting some help from a counter-current on the southern edge of the Gulf Stream, because when my fixes said that I should have covered, say, 150 miles, I sometimes found I had in fact logged 160 or 170.

'Of course, one of Tom's problems was that his log packed up half way over, so he couldn't do that check. The whole point is that it is much easier to find the edge of the Gulf Stream on the north side than it is to the south. On the northern edge you get warm water in the stream meeting cold water from the Labrador current. It is easy to know where you are by checking the temperature and sometimes you can even see a difference in the colour of the water. But on the south side you have warm water meeting warm water and that makes it much more difficult. That's where your experience comes in.'

Howell certainly played the Azores route game very well considering that it was his first attempt. He was actually past the Azores when the two French trimarans *Cap 33* and *Architeuthis* were still going through them, and he was in close contention with Jean-Marie Vidal until the bigger yacht suddenly opened her stride at the end of the first week of July.

Further north, the crucial days as far as the outcome of the race was concerned were the last in June, because until 27 June Jean-Yves Terlain was keeping *Vendredi 13* ahead of his main rival Alain Colas. Then they met in mid-ocean and Colas began to draw away. I don't want here to take the edge off Colas' dramatic story, but it is worth noting that although he was afraid *Vendredi* might well have made up the difference between them soon after their mid-ocean meeting, in fact *Pen Duick IV* did much better in the next few days and opened up the gap which was to prove vital to success.

In one way, the weather in the 1972 race was much more neutral than it had been for the previous runnings. Few singlehanders found really terrible conditions after the first ten days. Most had periods of frustrating calms. The fog and mist seemed to spread through the fleet just about evenly, and the irritations of getting through the light winds off Rhode Island Sound seemed to be common to all. Perhaps Bill Howell can again give us some indication of what a difference it made to him after 1968 – and going a different route.

'Last time, going along the northern route, I made 210 sail changes. That worked out at about nine a day. This time, going along the Azores route, I did 45 sail changes altogether. It works out at about 2½ a day. I spent most of the time getting a sun tan!'

And those dreaded icebergs? Few saw them, though Jock Brazier did report one monster when he was about half way across. 'I saw this huge thing coming over the horizon and it looked just like a block of flats,' he said in Newport. 'I didn't get too close to it obviously, but I think at a conservative estimate it must have been at least 150 feet high, maybe even as high as 300 feet.'

Chris Baranowski in *Polonez* thinks he may well have been in among the bergs too. He had a special water thermometer which electronically recorded the temperature outside the hull of his boat, and on several occasions he noticed a marked and rapid drop. But since he was going through thick fog at the time he couldn't tell if it was because of icebergs or not. 'And even if it was caused by an iceberg there was nothing very much I could do about it, so I just used to ignore it and go to sleep.'

Mike McMullen in *Binkie II* kept well to the north too, and he was quite convinced that he had been in the middle of the icebergs even though he had not seen any. 'I was so bloody frightened that I hove to for five hours on one occasion,' he told me when he arrived. Echoes of Leslie Williams' experience four years earlier: he hove to for half an hour in much the same circumstances.

Certainly the combination of icebergs and fog seems to have been far more menacing to the 1972 competitors who kept up near the great circle route than any ferocity of wind. And if it wasn't the ice–fog combination, it was the ships–fog danger. Quite apart from Bill Howell's disaster, several other sailors reported narrow squeaks. McMullen was convinced that he had very nearly been run down close to the Brenton Reef on the night he arrived. Marie-Claude Fauroux had been very worried in the same area. Baranowski and Linski both reported that there was a mass of shipping just when they were trying to edge their way home through the all-enveloping fog.

But even the best of sailors can make mistakes with regard to other shipping, even in fair conditions. Tom Follett wasn't saying much about his little adventure in Newport, but I did manage to discover that he had very nearly done what Eric Tabarly did in 1968. On the second day out from Plymouth he was making good progress and went below to make himself some coffee. He seemed to have been down no time at all when a sudden hoot brought him on deck fast, and there was a big cargo boat just veering away from *Three Cheers*. By the time Follett had got to the helm and released the steering the danger was over, but the big ship had passed far too close to *Three Cheers* for comfort.

But every Observer race has had its ration of this kind of story. Indeed they are the salt and pepper to the many wholesome stories that are told 'when the long trick's over'. It would certainly be a very dull race without them.

Considering the size of the fleet, the super-dramatic moments of the 1972 Observer Singlehanded were mercifully few. That any yacht should have to withdraw from the race is sad; that any yachtsman should suffer injury or illness is worse. But if one remembers the high incidence of dangerous moments in the 1968 race, when 35 yachts began the course, the comparatively low number of dramas in 1972, out of a starting fleet of 55, can only be cause for rejoicing.

Of course, those that suffered most probably found little reason for celebration. One can only feel great sympathy with someone like Bob Miller, who had to abandon his boat in mid-ocean. One can but mourn for Bill Howell, robbed of fifth place in the race by a bitter twist of fate. And one can feel nothing but compassion for Sir Francis Chichester's sad end to his attempt to win the race for the second time.

Inevitably, it was the Francis Chichester story which made the biggest headlines. He started the race easily the best-known of all the entrants. When he returned to Plymouth, beaten by the frailty of his 70-year-old body rather than by the might of the Atlantic, his name was even more renowned throughout the world.

The Chichester drama began within days of the start. Sir Francis had signed a contract to send special messages to *The Sunday Times* by radio. But they never materialised. The Swiss Guy Piazzini spoke to the skipper of *Gipsy Moth V* on Monday 19 June and heard that he was 'very tired' after the Saturday night gale, but the rest was silence.

No weekend call to *The Sunday Times*, no midweek check messages. Special transmissions just after the weather forecast broadcast failed to get a response from *Gipsy Moth V* and suspicion quickly mushroomed into rumour as everyone thought back to the frail figure that had dejectedly clambered forward to untangle that flapping jib. A mere nine days passed between Piazzini's message and the sighting of *Gipsy Moth V* by the 8,000-ton British cargo ship *Barrister* about 600 miles south-west of Land's End. But in that time every kind of mournful

prediction had been made about the old singlehander. Fortunately they were all wrong.

Chichester had actually decided to give up the race within a week of the start. He had given himself a pain-killing drug on 23 June. Next day he was feeling so sick, after a very bad night, that he decided to turn back for Plymouth. He explained later that he was by that time heading for the Azores and he thought the only thing to do was to head away from the islands because if he had been laid out the yacht would have stood on under her self-steering and perhaps sailed into the land.

Then one of the wires controlling the servo-rudder for his self-steering broke and to make *Gipsy Moth V* more manageable he decided to drop the mizzen staysail – what the British newspapers persisted in calling his mainsail long after the mistake had been pointed out. On 26 June Sir Francis did not feel strong enough to tackle the repair, so it was left to the next day – the day he was spotted by the British boat. As it happened, he had allowed *Gipsy Moth V* to go round on the other tack while he worked at the control wire, so the cargo boat saw him apparently on course for the Azores route to Newport.

But when RAF Nimrod aircraft followed up the ship's sighting with a flight over *Gipsy Moth V*, the old man found it difficult and tiring to signal to them, since they swept by so quickly. Eventually he sent the fateful message that he was weak and tired – to explain that he no longer wanted to carry on trying to get a message to them. Naturally when that poignant phrase was relayed back to the worried watchers in Britain it seemed especially pathetic against the background of missing messages and reports of a restricted sail-plan. It was all too easy to imagine that Chichester was seriously ill and in vital need of help.

Another message to another Nimrod was interpreted as meaning that Sir Francis wanted to meet his son Giles and John Anderson (the same J R L Anderson of *The Ulysses Factor*, who had joined *The Sunday Times* staff to take Chichester's messages during the race) in Brest. This was later found to be a mistaken reading. But the message to a circling plane on Wednesday 28 June was plain enough. It read 'I have been ill . . . I am OK'.

Nevertheless, *The Sunday Times* seemed concerned to get Giles Chichester and John Anderson to *Gipsy Moth V* and on Friday 30 June Giles was called away from his favourite sport – the rowing at Henley – and flown with Anderson to Culdrose, the naval air station just outside Helston in Cornwall. There they went into a navy Sea King helicopter together with cine cameramen representing BBC and independent television and an official navy photographer and headed out towards HMS *Salisbury*, a Royal Navy frigate which had been steaming back towards Plymouth when the alarm was raised.

I was in Plymouth that Friday morning and hasty telephone calls to London indicated that as a representative of the sponsoring newspaper I, too, should be allowed to go out in the Sea King. I drove off to Culdrose at rather more speed than I would normally have dared in the howling wind and rain which swept the winding roads of Cornwall. Still, I arrived in time to catch the helicopter, only to find that the Admiralty orders had not got through to Culdrose and I was not allowed aboard the flight.

But if I suffered a minor frustration, Sir Francis experienced a much worse one that same day. Around dawn he was asleep below when he heard a hooting. It was the French weather ship *France II*, anxious to give assistance.

Sir Francis signalled 'I am OK thanks' several times and when he saw the crew starting to pull back inboard a rubber dinghy they had seemed intent on launching he thought the ship was bearing away, so he went below. Then came another hoot and when he looked out the *France II* was almost alongside *Gipsy Moth V* and a man on the bridge was demanding to know where Sir Francis was heading. This obviously had become important because of the confusion about that message indicating Brest as a target.

He shouted 'Plymouth, Plymouth' and hoped the weather ship would then bear away and leave him to get on with his sailing. But the ship stood on and started to cross *Gipsy Moth*'s bows. Sir Francis had no time to free his self-steering and change course – he could only stand and pray there would be no collision. In vain, for the crosstrees of *Gipsy Moth V*'s

mizzen mast caught in the flanges of a row of portholes on *France II*, snapping the shrouds and bending the top of the mizzen mast.

Still anxious to help, the *France II* launched a boat which came across to *Gipsy Moth V* and from which Sir Francis was asked if he needed a doctor. He said that he didn't, but his boat might need one now!

After the *France II* had actually steamed away from the area the top 8 feet of the mizzen mast snapped off and ripped up the sail. So now even if he had wanted to sail back to Plymouth there was little hope of the old mariner managing the trip without some expert assistance first.

Fortunately, it was not far away. Friday evening Giles Chichester and Anderson were winched down on the *Salisbury* and she steamed towards *Gipsy Moth V*'s position about 180 miles off the French coast. They found the yacht at about three in the morning, and at first light could see that the damage was extensive. When Sir Francis came on deck HMS *Salisbury* closed to within hailing distance and her skipper, Commander McQueen, ask if Sir Francis would like Giles and Anderson to cross to the yacht.

The answer was 'yes' so the transfer began. Later a rigging specialist went aboard to tidy up the mizzen mast mess and then, when John Anderson returned to *Salisbury*, the Chichesters were joined by Lt-Commander Peter Martin – an experienced offshore racing helmsman – and two other naval technicians. With this crew the crippled *Gipsy Moth V* eventually returned to Plymouth, where Sir Francis was taken to hospital.

It emerged later that though he had given up hope of getting to Newport, Sir Francis was quite prepared to complete the voyage back to Plymouth without assistance. Indeed, but for the incident with *France II* he would almost certainly have insisted upon it. The *France II* actually had a disastrous day that Friday. After leaving *Gipsy Moth V*, she continued on her way towards France and then was in collision with the American yacht *Lefteria* – also sailing towards *Gipsy Moth V* to see if Sir Francis needed help. The damage this time was worse than a broken mast.

The *Lefteria* sank; four of her crew were rescued and one body recovered; the other six members went missing. Later Sir Francis wrote in *The Sunday Times* 'I want to say how sorry I am at the grievous loss of life from the yacht *Lefteria* . . . this news came as a dreadful shock. I had not asked for help, but that cannot alter the fact that those who lost their lives were trying to help me. They acted in the highest tradition of the sea, and I am deeply distressed that their generous action ended so disastrously.'

When H M S *Salisbury* returned to Plymouth late on the night of Saturday 1 July, it was possible to fit together some of the pieces still missing from the puzzle. It emerged that the radio on *Gipsy Moth V* had been capable of receiving but not transmitting – hence the inexplicable silence of the old man of the sea. And Commander McQueen told me that the skipper was actually looking remarkably fit and not in need of any medical assistance.

The big ketch followed *Salisbury* in to Plymouth on the Monday after, by which time Sir Francis was already smiling and waving happily to his well-wishers. Lt-Commander Martin reported that he had been very tired and very relieved to see the help arrive. 'But he has no intention of retiring, and told me he already had another voyage in mind.' From hints dropped by Giles Chichester, this seemed likely to be a new speed solo sailing record. There appeared to be no end to the adventurous endeavour of this remarkable man.

The postscript to the Chichester drama was written a couple of weeks later, when it was announced that the Ministry of Defence had asked *The Sunday Times* to contribute to the £3,000 spent by the R A F and Royal Navy on the rescue operation. Mr Peter Kirk, Under-Secretary of State, Defence, told the House of Commons that his department was in touch with the newspaper about a contribution to costs in answer to questions by two Labour members.

Mr Marcus Lipton, M P for Brixton, said – without actually mentioning Sir Francis – 'it is abominable that public money should be spent through the vanity and obstinacy of foolhardy persons who seem willing to lend themselves to commercially sponsored exploitation'. The old cry, which is bound to go up every time the services become involved in a rescue operation such as this. It seems that few of the complainers ever consider the services' own attitude to such exercises.

Commander McQueen told me that even though the extra voyage out to *Gipsy Moth V* meant delayed

shore leave for most of his ship's company, everyone aboard *Salisbury* was eager to go to the aid of Sir Francis. And finding a small yacht like that in the middle of the ocean, at night, was a good test of search and rescue capabilities that added considerably to the ship's experience.

Certainly all the service personnel I spoke to during the whole exercise – both at Culdrose and in Plymouth – seemed to welcome the chance to test their skills in a situation that really could have been a matter of life or death.

I wonder if some Russian official started asking awkward questions in the Kremlin about the part played by the Russian fishing vessels of Rhode Island Sound in the rescue of Bill Howell and his catamaran *Tahiti Bill*. Somehow I doubt it.

The *Tahiti Bill* drama was, in its own way, just as poignant as the rescue of *Gipsy Moth V*, though there was little poignancy about the always-laughing, quite unabashed Bill Howell when he eventually arrived in Newport. He actually had every reason to be pleased with his performance in the race, for had he not been involved in a collision a mere 100 miles from the finish line he would have finished fifth in the race and would have made good his promise to take a week off his 1968 time of $31\frac{1}{2}$ days.

And that would have meant beating *Pen Duick IV* to the handicap trophy for multihulls – no mean achievement in a 43-foot cruising catamaran. But it was not to be. *Tahiti Bill* slammed into the Russian trawler *Spika* just south of Nantucket Light Vessel in thick fog at 6.30 pm on 12 July.

Experienced seaman that he is, Howell's first reaction was to check the amount of damage and see if there was any danger of sinking. In fact the collision had crumpled the prow of the port float of *Tahiti Bill* and ripped open the hull, but fortunately there is a watertight bulkhead across the float and this prevented the water getting any further. So the cat was merely listing slightly to port but quite steady. Then the skipper noticed that the mast was wobbling about, so he secured that with jury rigging.

By the time the fishing boat had lifted its trawl and come close to see if any help were needed, Howell had decided that he might get the crippled boat home and had raised a mainsail and jib. 'But the hole in the hull kept filling up and I was dead scared of the bulkhead giving way,' he told me in Newport. 'Plus it was still dense fog, and if she had gone down I could have been out there in a rubber dinghy for days.'

So Howell accepted the offer of assistance from the Russian fleet supply ship *Flotinspekcija*. This arrived about dawn on 13 June and took *Tahiti Bill* in tow – from the stern in order to avoid increasing the pressure on that bulkhead. The Australian transferred to the Russian ship and, after some delaying tactics, was eventually allowed to use the supply vessel's radio to call up the US Coast Guard and relate what had happened.

I listened transfixed to the exchange of messages as I sat in Newport, feeling deeply sorry for a very tired-sounding Howell but occasionally being prompted to smile at the very guarded manoeuvrings between the representatives of two nations with no great love for each other. For example, when Howell reported that he was being towed towards Newport by the Russian supply ship, the Coast Guards advised him that the alien vessel should not come any closer than the three-mile limit. Howell promptly replied that the Russian skipper had no intention of coming any closer than the 12-mile limit!

But it was all resolved amicably. The *Point Turner*, an 80-foot Coast Guard cutter, took over the tow some 50 miles from Newport and the stricken catamaran eventually arrived late on the Thursday evening, with her Australian skipper amazingly cheerful, considering the events of the previous 24 hours. Somebody asked him if he were injured at all and he replied with a laugh, 'No injuries – but me nerves were a bit bad to start with.'

Howell then told us that he could have avoided the collision if he had passed north of the light vessel. He knew where it was and could have left it to port quite easily and safely. But knowing that was against the rules he tacked and came round it, thinking he would be over the line by noon the next day (13 June) and certain to take the multihull handicap prize.

'Then whang – I hit it. I didn't see it and it didn't see me. They told me they had looked at the radar 20 minutes before and not seen me. And I didn't hear a fog horn, though it's very difficult to hear a horn in those conditions. I was doing about seven knots at the time, but the impact was worse than

that because I think the trawler tried to veer away and her stern was actually swinging round towards me when we hit.

'Of course, up to that point I was doing very well. I had taken the Azores route and had got to the islands in nine days – though it was a bit rough coming out of the Channel. Then I came along the southern edge of the Gulf Stream and was making good time apart from about 36 hours when I was becalmed about half way across. When I cut across the Gulf Stream I hit a big gale on the northern edge, but I kept going at about four knots to windward.'

Howell had obviously sailed an exceptionally skilful race and deserved a much better fate. He had heard on the radio that Alain Colas was home and he knew he had six days to beat the big trimaran on handicap – and would have been home in five. In fact, Colas was one of the first to greet him at Newport, saying what great sympathy he had for the Australian. 'Another time, another year,' said the Frenchman. 'Yeah,' replied Howell, 'we'll change boats.' And the joyous laughter was quite undimmed.

When Jack Odling-Smee arrived to add his condolences, the irrepressible Aussie, who had voiced many good-natured complaints about the race committee's attitude to sponsored boats, reminded the Colonel that he had promised him a dance in Newport. 'Jack said he would dance with me on the deck of *Vendredi 13*, drinking Cap Export beer and Strongbow cider, while smoking Peter Stuyvesant cigarettes,' he shouted. And his full-blooded Sydney-twanged laugh rang out over the dockside at Port O'Call. There wasn't one among us who didn't admire the humour and courage of a man who could react so cheerfully in such a situation.

Thinking back to that sighting of the Russian fleet we made on the flight out to find *Vendredi 13* the previous Friday, I was not surprised that they should form a considerable hazard in bad weather conditions. Colas told me that he had sailed through them at night, but in good clear conditions, and Brian Cooke reported some qualms when he crossed the same stretch of water. Both Mike McMullen and Marie-Claude Fauroux came through the danger area when there was lots of fog about and said that they had heard an alarming number of fog horns, though they had seen nothing. It seems that the Russian fleet represents a new hazard in the closing stages of the race, never the easiest part of the voyage in the light airs of Rhode Island Sound and made especially dangerous in 1972 by the persistent fog that obscured the area for much of July.

It wasn't fog that caused the other casualties. Mostly it was too much wind, for a rash of broken masts told their own story. Two came soon after the start on 17 June – to Max Barton's *Bristol Fashion* and Richard Konkolski's *Nike*. Barton was able to get his repaired quite quickly and set out again from Plymouth on 26 June. For Konkolski the problem was more acute. *Nike* is a tiny yawl (just 22·5 feet) to his own design, so a replacement was not an easy thing to find. However, despite a charming letter to Port O'Call Marina saying how sad he was that he wouldn't be sailing to America after all, the Czech set out again from Plymouth on 29 June.

But there was not much hope of re-starting for Gerard Dijkstra and the big 71-foot ketch *Second Life*. He lost his main mast in a very sudden blow that whipped up to force 9 on 1 July. The accident happened when the Dutchman was about 650 miles east of St John, New Brunswick, at a time when *Second Life* was well up with the leaders.

Fortunately, Dijkstra was able to get a tow to St John's, Newfoundland, scene of Alain Gliksman's sad withdrawal from the 1968 race. The photographs which came back to us from there showed a disconsolate Dijkstra and his wife Loomtje staring sadly at the jagged stump of the huge mast. It had snapped off right at the base and gone clean overboard without damaging any other part of the boat. Thus ended the challenge of yet another of the fancied boats.

Bob Miller's *Mersea Pearl* may not have been considered a serious contender for the outright honours, but it probably attracted as much, if not more, publicity than the favourites. For bandleader Bob was a household name anyway, and the tremendous promotion given to his entry by the BBC made sure that millions of radio listeners knew all about his transatlantic sail.

In the early days of the race Miller's live radio reports to the Tony Brandon lunchtime pop music programme worked extremely well. The single-hander sounded confident and cheerful and he was making very good progress in his Carter-designed sloop. A clear indication of how his adventure had caught the imagination of the radio listeners came when Tony Brandon announced the results of a competition to guess how many miles Miller had sailed in the first six days of the race. No less than 10,000 post-cards had flooded into Broadcasting House, London.

But then came the tragedy. Two-thirds of the way across the ocean (on 10 July) when *Mersea Pearl* was about 500 miles south-east of St John's, 'there was a sudden crack and the mast broke away' – as Miller described it later. 'The sea was rough and it was pitch black. I could hear the mast hitting the side of the hull as the waves pounded us, and I had to hang on for grim life as I chopped away the shrouds which still connected the mast to the boat.'

When at last the mast was clear Miller realised that it had taken his radio aerial with it, so he pulled a plank of wood from the cabin, drilled three holes in it and managed to screw it to the side of the boat. It was no more than 9 feet high, but it did enable the musician mariner to raise Portishead Radio. 'They were fantastic,' he said. 'They could just about hear me, although their signals to me were loud and clear.'

Portishead alerted the nearest ship, the *Hoegh Minerva*. She is a Norwegian bulk carrier of nearly 16,000 tons and at the time she was near Miller's position on course for Middlesbrough. The *Hoegh Minerva* took Miller aboard and put a tow on *Mersea Pearl*, but she had to maintain her normal speed of 15 knots and that proved too much for the tow line and the fragile hull of *Mersea Pearl*. 'Shortly after, the yacht started taking water fast. The tow broke and the last I saw of her she was slowly going down. She didn't sink in my view, but she must be down now.'

A sad story to have to tell, but Bob Miller didn't seem too depressed by it when he returned to Britain, for all that he had lost the boat which had cost him £19,000 to buy and prepare for this race. And the experience of competing in the Observer Single-handed, even if he did not finish, seemed to mark a turning point in his life, for on his return he announced that he had resolved to quit the hectic life of a bandleader and find some other occupation which did not make such demands on his personal life – and maybe allow him more time for sailing as well.

That Murray Sayle should fail to finish the course

in *Lady of Fleet* was a great sadness; not only to those with a vested interest in his success, like *The Sunday Times* and the BBC, but to all those who enjoyed his sparkling reports to *The Times* and its Sunday associate. Sayle brought out a new dimension of single-handing – he captured brilliantly all the little worries, distractions, boredoms, frustrations, and delights of a long solo sail. He made every reader aware of how it felt to spend your last night in port before setting out on a transatlantic adventure. He conveyed exactly the heightened perceptions of a man who has been at sea for weeks on end with only the infinite excursions of his own mind for company.

Until its disastrous end, Sayle's was indeed a long solo sail. He had chosen the Azores route and was unfortunate enough to get becalmed for the best part of a fortnight near the islands. In Newport, where Peter Dunning made a meticulous point of running up the flag of the latest finisher's country, there was good-natured chaff about running up a Christmas tree complete with lights by the time 'Sea-dog Sayle' (as Bill Howell called him) got to the finishing line.

But in fact *Lady of Fleet* had made quite good progress in the second third of her passage across the ocean. When her main mast broke she was actually 820 miles north-west of Bermuda and her skipper was reckoning that he would finish about ten days later. Sayle's description of the calamity, which appeared in *The Sunday Times* on 30 July, has a dramatic economy that could not be bettered.

'I woke just before 2 am. The wind was down to eight knots but the swell was heavier, the blue hills of the afternoon were now black mountains, and a huge black cloud covered the sky. In a minute or two it began to rain, a cloudburst hissing down on the sea. I got into oilskins, deck boots, and safety harness and stood in the cockpit, puzzling over the instruments which report the wind's speed and direction and the yacht's heading and speed.

'Suddenly the rain stopped as if shut off by a tap, the wind speed dropped to 20 knots and the boat's speed to five. Both speeds hovered for a moment on the dials and then the wind speed needle started to climb fast – to 30, 35, 40. At exactly 40 knots the main mast crumpled 6 feet above the deck like a broken match. Mast, genoa, and mainsail went over the side.'

It had all happened within 10 seconds. Sayle had turned to the main sheet but the mast had gone before he could release it. His choice then was to cut the mast adrift or try to secure it. He chose the latter course, mainly because he knew he could then salvage his radio aerial. With the mast secured alongside, he rigged the aerial to the mizzen mast and raised Ocean Gate, the US Coast Guard's station near New York.

It happened that the Coast Guard cutter *Chase* was 100 miles north of *Lady of Fleet*, on her way back to America after a training cruise to Britain and Norway with 52 cadets aboard. Because she had called at the Azores to refuel she was closer to Murray Sayle than any singlehander would have a right to expect in that area of the ocean which is not normally used by commercial shipping.

The dismasting had happened at two. By 3.30 am Sayle was talking to the *Chase*. A rendezvous was arranged for 2.30 pm and at 2.25, when the Australian put his head out for a look, 'a white ship with a cheerful red, white, and blue stripe was bearing down on me, perhaps a mile away. It was the *Chase*.'

So *Lady of Fleet* was taken in tow, looking, as Sayle described her, 'like a pretty girl with her teeth punched in'. Still able to see the ironic twist to this sort of situation, Sayle reports his conversation with *Chase*'s skipper. ' "It will have to be where we are going," he said. "We are bound for Newport, Rhode Island." '

The Solaris cat survived well. Apart from the mast she was completely seaworthy at the end of her chequered trip across the ocean. And her voyage had certainly added a lot to the literature of single-handed sailing.

The other withdrawals were, happily, less dramatic. Harry Mitchell's brave effort to get the little *Tuloa* across the ocean ended just two days after the start when she sprung a leak that would have made a transatlantic passage a perilous affair. He was the second to retire, after *Oscar Debra*.

Eugene Riguidel's answer to those exhortations, 'Allez Eugene!' were almost as short-lived. He returned to France on 25 June with rigging failure. Edoardo Guzzetti called it a day on 29 June when he simply felt too ill to continue. The American Jerry Cartwright had to put *Scuffler III* into Falmouth soon after the start because she was leaking, but he sailed again on 27 June. Andrew Spedding's *Summersong* re-entered the race three days earlier

*Mid-ocean meeting. HMS Salisbury sails
close to Gipsy Moth V and Giles Chichester
prepares to lead a naval party across to help his
father repair the battered mizzen mast of
Gipsy Moth V.*
Photo: Tony McGrath

As Alain Colas drops the sails on Pen Duick IV, his Tahitian fiancée Teura Krause can hardly contain her delight that the trimaran which had been her home for so many hundred miles has actually crossed the line first.
Photo: Chris Smith

Exultation shines in the face of Alain Coles as he arrives at the Port O'Call Marina in Newport, knowing that he is at last winner of the 1972 Observer Singlehanded race.
Photo: Chris Smith

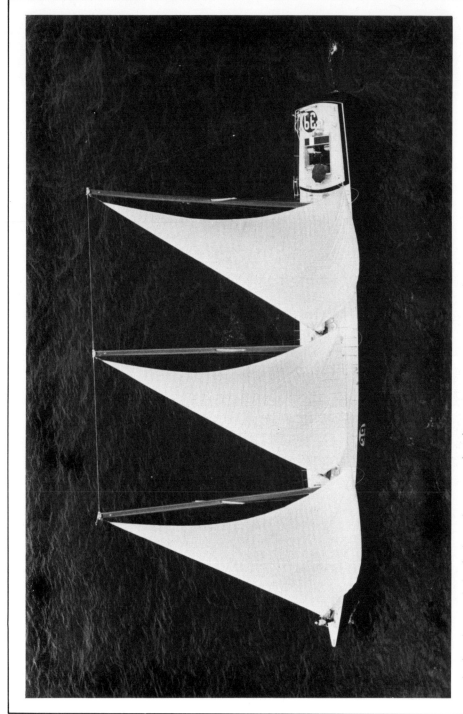

As she ghosted across Rhode Island Sound,
Vendredi 13 made good use of her three huge
genoas, dwarfing Jean-Yves Terlain as he
stood on the prow.
Photo: Chris Smith

Jean-Marie Vidal gets Cap 33 shipshape after the long haul, looking justifiably pleased with his third place overall.
Photo: Frank Page

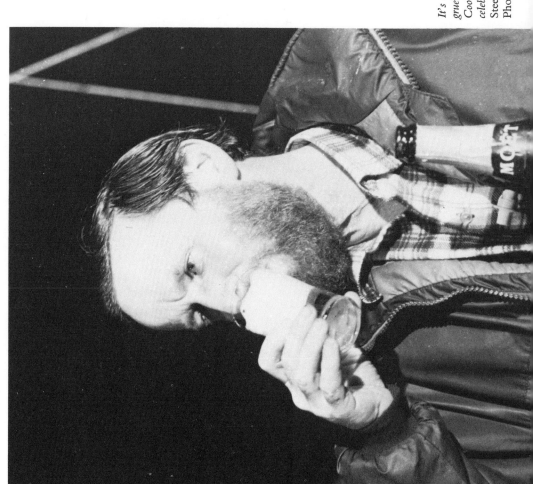

It's 4 o'clock in the morning, at the end of a gruelling twenty-five-day sail, but Brian Cooke can still relish a glass of champagne to celebrate finishing in fourth place in British Steel.

Photo: Frank Page

Three Cheers, exceptionally fast when she can find wind, ties up alongside at Newport. Her construction is very strong, yet light, and gear was kept to a functional minimum.

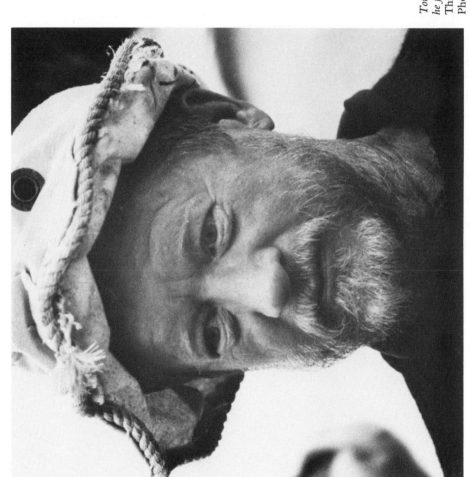

Tom Follett's face reflects all the disappointment he felt making a depressingly slow crossing in Three Cheers.
Photo: Frank Page

Night arrival. Gerard Pestey's big trimaran Architeuthis is edged up to the quay at the Port O'Call Marina, Newport, having crossed from Plymouth in the remarkably quick time of twenty-seven and a half days.

Photo: Frank Page

A forest of masts in Newport. At the end of the trip comes peace, tranquillity and the chance to dry out gear. A spinnaker balloons from Chris Baranowski's Polonez and alongside her is Linski's Isles du Frioul. Behind lie British Steel, Flying Angel and Wild Rocket. Photo: Frank Page

Centre of attention, Alain Colas puzzles over the probing questions of the press and television interviewers.

Photo: Frank Page

Teura Krause reflects Alain Colas' unabashed delight in victory as she points her Tahitian toes along the outriggers of Pen Duick IV.
Photo: Frank Page

The Black Pearl is a sailing oriented restaurant in Newport where many a post-mortem was held after the race. Here the first two men home compare their routes across the ocean.

Photo: Chris Smith

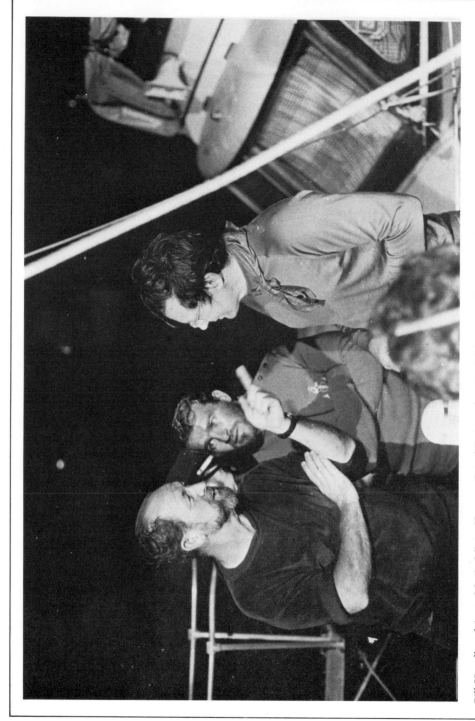

Bill Howell explains to Martin Minter-Kemp how, if only he hadn't hit that Russian trawler, his catamaran Tahiti Bill would have been home quite a while before Strongbow.

Gerard Pestey, whose English is very good, strains to unravel the Australian accent.

Photo: Chris Smith

When Alain Gliksman arrived at Newport with the skinny little Toucan, it seemed incredible that he could have sailed her faster than lots of boats half as long again. A worthy winner of the trophy for boats up to 35 feet. Photo: Chris Smith

Face of the victor. Alain Colas smiles tiredly after sailing Pen Duick IV to victory in 20 days, 13 hours and 15 minutes.

after repairs had been effected following the minor collision he experienced when sailing down towards Land's End.

The other boat was another competitor in the race, it seems, but Spedding was not telling who it was. 'I could have killed him at the time,' he told me with some venom in his voice.

The first casualty, Joel Charpentier's *Wild Rocket*, eventually made up enough time to finish 16th in Newport, but the return to Plymouth, plus a fairly tough handicap allowance, put him out of the running for any other honours. Indeed, for much of the later period of the race, when the middle-size boats were arriving at Newport, *Wild Rocket* languished at the bottom of the monohull handicap list.

Saturday 5 August turned out to be a sad day for the makers of the Listang boats. It was on that day that we heard that both Bob Salmon's *Justa Listang* and Max Barton's *Bristol Fashion* had lost their masts – Barton's for the second time. Fortunately both skippers were unharmed.

A message from Lloyd's told us that Salmon and his yacht had been taken aboard the Swedish motor vessel *Traviata* on that Saturday, four days after her dismasting. At that time *Traviata* was heading for Drammen, near Oslo in Norway.

Max Barton's second dismasting was rather earlier, on 26 July. Barton was met by the German vessel *Dalbek* on 5 August, which supplied the Bristol man with food for the return journey to Plymouth under jury rig. When the mast broke he was 500 miles south of Cape Race and thus well on the way to Newport. He told the German ship he thought that at the rate he could sail under the improvised rig, he would probably get back to England on 14 September.

The same weekend we heard that Carlo Mascheroni, whose *Chica Boba* had been strangely missing from our charts, had in fact given up quite early in the race. He had sailed off south to Gibraltar and from there returned to his home in Milan. Thus only two of the four Italian entries completed the course.

12 Pen Duick again

Friday, 7th July, dawned bright and sunny in Newport, Rhode Island, and Chris Smith and I worked out that it just had to be the day when things started happening. As we sipped coffee in the Seamen's Church Institute we tried to analyse all the probabilities and decide on a course of action. That was not as easy as one might think, looking back on the race with the knowledge of who finished when and what the relative positions were in mid-ocean.

We were trying to make out the picture on the jig-saw puzzle while many of the pieces remained missing. We knew that Terlain had radioed a position that morning which put him about 50 miles from the Nantucket light vessel, in turn about 110 miles from the finishing line at Brenton Tower. It seemed almost certain that he would be the first boat home, but we were worried about the lack of news from *Pen Duick IV*.

Making all sorts of guesstimates from the meagre information we had received about the big trimaran's progress, we thought it was either close on *Vendredi 13*'s heels or possibly just ahead. Then, of course, there was always the possibility that Tom Follett in *Three Cheers* would come sneaking in unheralded, as he had done four years earlier.

The Observer was obviously expecting a story from us. Saturday's deadlines for the Sunday paper seemed uncomfortably close. We had to make a definite move. So we began to talk about taking an aeroplane out to sea. But could we be sure to find the big schooner? And if we did, could we be certain that she really was in front of all the opposition? At 160 miles offshore the sea becomes a very big place and a tiny yacht can so easily be missed, even from 2,500 feet in good visibility.

But *Vendredi* was not exactly a tiny yacht and our fix on her seemed very exact. It meant that she would have to be sailing west and slightly south to round the light ship before turning north-west again for Newport, so we felt confident that we could fly along her track and make a sighting. The decision made, we headed out to Newport's small and informal airport and soon the cameras were being loaded into an Air Commander.

Our aim was to find Terlain and establish his likely finishing time, then sweep the approaches to Newport to make sure that no other yacht could beat him to the line. And when we returned we were convinced we had done just that. Only later did we realise how dangerous it is to make any sort of assumption about sea and boats, or indeed about the Observer Singlehanded race.

Our course out to sea was simple to set. We passed over the Brenton Tower and caught a glimpse of the white breakers on Brenton Reef, then headed straight for the Nantucket light vessel. After all the brouhaha of Geoffrey Williams and *Sir Thomas Lipton* going north of the light four years earlier, we knew that no competitor in this race would be planning to cut any corners, so that simplified matters.

On the way out we passed a large fleet of fishing vessels. Russians, we were told, and we looked down on them interestedly. We were not to know then that those Russian trawlers would play a big part in a later drama of the race.

And then we saw her – a flash of white sail against the grey-blue of the glassy, glistening ocean. It was *Vendredi*, exactly where she should have been, making a direct course for the light vessel under her three billowing genoas. In the sharp morning sunlight she looked absolutely magnificent, though she was not making very good time, for the wind was only about force 3 and those three big sails were drawing but fitfully.

Still, she was making 2 to 3 knots, and that brought to mind the interesting debate about the light weather sails. Designer Dick Carter had said he wanted to keep the sail plan of the huge boat absolutely simple. He thought the overwhelming length of the design would make up for any lack of variety in the sail locker. The three boomed staysails would give forward drive in all but very light airs, he contended, and to provide any more sails would only be an invitation to the singlehander to overtax his strength and thus defeat the object.

But Terlain himself was not convinced. He ordered the three genoas and had them fitted just in time for the race. That first sighting we made of *Vendredi* seemed immediately to justify all his thinking. In those conditions, under the staysails, the schooner would barely have been moving. With the three creamy genoas ballooning gently over the long hull she was creeping quietly but inevitably towards the finishing line. She was then a mere 20 miles from the light ship and it seemed she must get to the line in about another day for certain victory.

But still there was that uneasy feeling that we ought to have sighted *Pen Duick IV* as well. So as we circled over *Vendredi 13*, I evolved a rough plan for the flight home. Chris was busy getting his pictures of Terlain, who had come up from below when he heard the aircraft circling and was looking at us just as intently (through his binoculars) as we were peering at him. From what we could see, he looked fit and well and the boat was immaculate. Gone now were the oilskins and crash hat. He was dressed simply in dark jeans, white sweater, and woollen cap. The only concession to comfort we could see as we circled was a small blue umbrella fixed over the cockpit to provide a measure of protection against rain or sun.

As the last shutter clicked I asked if we could return to Newport along a line well to the south of the light vessel, just in case *Pen Duick* was off in that direction somewhere. We kept our eyes skinned all the way back, but no sign. So when we found Terlain's backer Claude Lelouch waiting for us at the airport, we were able to give him good news without any hesitation.

The French film-maker had decided to abandon the idea of producing a movie called 'A Man and a Boat' to follow on the success of his earlier 'A Man and a Woman' but he was still intensely keen to see his man home first. I told him we had seen the big schooner gliding along majestically. 'Et *Pen Duick*?' he asked. 'No sign,' I replied, and he grinned an eager, boyish grin and held up both hands to heaven, eight of the ten fingers firmly crossed.

Now Chris Smith wanted to get his films back to London by air and I was anxious to put my copy on a Telex machine, so we hopped into the Triumph Stag which had been loaned to me by British Leyland's North American company and headed for Boston.

We returned only just in time. As I nosed the Stag back into the crowded parking area outside the Port o'Call Marina there were people rushing everywhere. We soon learned the reason why. Alain Colas and *Pen Duick IV* had been sighted just off the finishing line. The race would go to the trimaran after all. Within minutes we had collected cameras, recording machines, notebooks, and all the other paraphernalia, and were aboard Jim Hayman's high-powered Chris Craft. We were just about to zoom out of the Marina and off to Brenton Tower when we saw Teura Krause, Alain Colas' beautiful Tahitian fiancée, running down the dock looking desperately for a boat. It took just a moment to get her aboard, and off we sped.

Even as we surged over the still evening water towards the tower there was some confusion. It seemed that Claude Lelouch, no doubt still with every finger crossed, had flown out himself that afternoon to make sure that Terlain would be the winner. One of his party in the plane wanted to photograph part of the coastline south of the normal approach to Newport so, having confirmed that the schooner was still sailing serenely on towards the finish, the plane swung off to the south.

And then they saw *Pen Duick*. At least, they thought it could only have been *Pen Duick* in that position at that time. So, even as we roared out to the finish line none of us was absolutely certain what we would find. Teura was an excited mixture of exultation and trepidation. 'Are you sure it is *Pen Duick*?' she asked. 'No, I am not,' I replied. 'See if you can see the boat.' Together we searched the horizon.

'There it is,' shouted a man from *Paris-Match*. 'It's *Treize*!' Teura's face fell and she peered even more intensely into the gathering gloom. 'No – there are two masts, not three. It is Alain!'

Now we could all see. It was indeed *Pen Duick*. And she was right at the line as we came up to her. Somehow a whole flotilla of small craft had heard the news in time to make the rendez-vous and most of them seemed to be full of French cameramen, journalists, friends, and television crews. Cheers and shouts of congratulations rang across the sea, some in English, but most in French. Flash-lights were popping, floodlights rose and fell in intensity as the television cameras snatched snippets of film, and through it all Alain Colas calmly went about dropping his sails and grinning delightedly.

He looked fit and tanned. When he smiled in

triumph for the cameras, which was often, his teeth dazzled in the fading evening light. There was a specially wide smile for our boat because Teura was standing on it, her beautiful big brown Polynesian eyes absolutely aglow with delight. 'Oh,' she said to me, 'I have forgotten to bring my welcoming present for Alain – a hai, the necklet of flowers that we put round the necks of visitors to Tahiti.'

I don't think Colas minded. He had enough happiness shining out of him to keep going for quite a long time. We put a line aboard *Pen Duick* and were about to tow her back to Newport when somebody saw the Coast Guard cutter rushing across to us. It had the custom man aboard as well as Jack Odling-Smee of the race committee, so we handed over the job to them and motored back to Port O'Call for the reception.

And what a reception it was! The dockside was thick with the waiting crowds and it seemed that every hooter and siren in Newport was sounding off as the grim grey shape of *Pen Duick* came into the glare of the BBC's special television floodlights. There was the victorious singlehander, line in hand, waiting to tie up after crossing 3,000 miles of the North Atlantic in the incredible time of 20 days, 13 hours, and 15 minutes.

First man to greet Colas in any kind of coherent manner, amidst the elbowing, shouting, demanding news and television men, was the Mayor of Newport who opened a bottle of champagne (Californian) and poured it into a glass (plastic). It was a pleasant gesture, which the Frenchman acknowledged gracefully, but he couldn't resist asking his young brother Jean-François to go aboard *Pen Duick* and bring out the celebratory bottle he had brought himself. This turned out to be no less than a magnum of Taittinger. Colas gleefully poured some and said to the mayor, 'I hope now you will have some French champagne.'

The French consul from Boston brought a special message of congratulations from the Ambassador in Washington, but not the immediate award of Chevalier of the Légion d'Honneur which was given to Colas' mentor Eric Tabarly when he won the 1964 race. I asked him why not and he replied, 'Ah well, you must understand. Tabarly was a serving officer of the French forces. It is an altogether different thing.'

By shaving nearly 5½ days off the record for the passage set by Geoffrey Williams in 1968, Colas had fulfilled Philip Weld's prophecy almost to the hour. Weld estimated the winner's time in 1972 as 500 hours. Colas actually made the crossing in just over 493. Weld said that the race would be won dinghy style – and that's exactly how Colas did it, spending long hours at the helm, urging every ounce of effort out of his boat, almost willing her to Newport ahead of the pack.

For much of the voyage he had no option, for it emerged as he talked to the Press men that his self-steering gear broke four days after he left Plymouth. He managed to effect a repair, but it lasted only five more days. Then it was damaged beyond Colas' repair capability, so he had to fit a replacement unit which was only capable of dealing with moderate going – at high speed or in light airs he just had to be at the helm.

He told us that he had in fact been at the helm for the greater part of the last three days before the finish, allowing himself only 3½ hours sleep in all that time. When I asked why so little, his reply put into a few words all his determination, and all his seamanship. It was the sort of answer you would expect from a man who had learned at the elbow of Eric Tabarly. 'I wanted to win and I was worried about other shipping. And, anyway, it's a matter of principle. When you get near the coast you do not behave stupidly.'

But it was when, at last, I was able to go below with Alain Colas, for the exclusive interview which he had agreed to give *The Observer*, that I really saw the skill, determination, and courage which had brought this man victory in the fourth Observer Singlehanded. He started by showing me the entry in his log for 27 June when he was almost exactly half way across the ocean. It was the only entry in a series of cryptic notes that used capital letters for emphasis. Little wonder, for this was how it read: '11th day, 27 June. Wind 11 to 12 knots and sea beautiful. TREIZE TWO MILES AHEAD! A little competition between Terlain and me. 15.40 – passed Terlain and celebrated by eating a tin of home-made peaches in syrup.'

It was an incredible coincidence. After sailing 1,500 miles into the Atlantic and in a situation where the two boats could be hundreds of miles apart to north or south, they were actually on exactly the same course. As Colas told me about it, his voice rose higher and higher and his eyes got wider and wider.

'To come upon him like that just in the middle of the ocean – it's unthinkable. One morning I was odd-jobbing on board and getting my sextant ready for a sight. I came on deck and I looked around me as I always do and I see a sailing boat! I see masts! I get the glasses and it was 13! I screamed, I just screamed. I rushed for the helm and I stayed there until I caught up with him. I only had my lunch at dinner time!'

It sounds slightly bathetic that Colas should add the comment about having to delay eating, when to beat Terlain obviously meant so much to him, but it's important to remember that the one indulgence Colas did allow himself in his otherwise rigidly strict routine was good food as often as possible. He took a supply of Norman food with him which sounds more appropriate to the Ritz restaurant than a singlehanded boat in mid-Atlantic – Camembert, Pont l'Eveque, and Livarot cheeses; pâté; Pripes à la mode de Caen and a supply of Calvados. 'He likes to eat well – like all Frenchmen,' says Teura. 'It helps to keep his spirits up.'

But let us allow the victor to finish the story of his mid-ocean conquest of the great rival. 'It was windward work in light airs. When I was with him it was roughly mid-morning and the noon fix put us exactly half way across. Exactly. It took almost the day to catch up with him, because I was going slightly faster, but we are both fast boats. I signalled to him and he stayed sit. Then he went below and then he came out again and went forward and sat in his balcony and looked at me. And then he waved and I waved back.'

In that simple, slightly ungrammatical description of the crisis moment of the whole 1972 Observer Singlehanded, one can almost feel the intense rivalry between the two youthful Frenchmen, almost hear the vital questions going round in their brains 1,500 miles from the start of their great adventure. Did this mean that Jean-Yves Terlain's long and successful campaign to raise enough money to build the biggest and most intimidating single-handed boat in man's history was to end in bitter defeat? Did it mean that Alain Colas' four years of absolute dedication to the ideal of winning this race at whatever cost to himself and his pretty girl-friend would at last be crowned with glory? Or was this just one crisis in a series of peak moments that would ultimately decide the great challenge?

We know now that it was indeed the turning point of the whole race, and we can also guess at the extra impetus it gave to Colas in his fierce determination to get his trimaran ahead and to stay ahead.

'I did not come up close to him,' the winner continued. 'To compare how my boat was faring with his I stayed exactly in his wake until I came close enough, and then I let her bear away a bit and passed to leeward, and kept going down to sort of widen the gap quickly. I thought if it had been me I would not like to see the other guy come luffing up and pass just ahead of my bows, so I steered away from him. I was going much faster but much farther to leeward. Then once I was well ahead of him I luffed up again.

'But I was not convinced I was ahead of him for the rest of the race. I had caught up with him – okay – but there was still a long way to go and the following day I was caught in calms, and I am certain that he tacked away from them. Next morning, when I could see the sea getting flat calm and could tell that we were going towards the blankest calm ever, I knew within myself that Terlain had certainly felt that and had tacked away, whereas I was feeling so happy-go-lucky for having passed him that I sort of kept going. And I knew we were roughly equal, so it was a matter of who would be first in Newport; who would sleep less; who would stay at the helm longer.'

As it turned out, Colas had no alternative but to stay at the helm for much of the time, because of his broken self-steering gear. 'The spare gear enabled me to get some sleep, get some food and do some navigation, but as far as getting the boat home to Newport – it had to be me,' he said.

Evidence enough, perhaps, of the tremendous determination to win that lies within the stocky frame of Alain Colas, but there were more details which brought out all the singlemindedness of this worthy race winner. For example, I asked him for some more information about how he repaired that self-steering gear.

'It was the connection underneath the hull between the gear and the rudder that went,' he told me. 'There was only one thing to do. I took the sails down, got my tools, fixed myself to the boat with a line and went overboard and fixed the rudder. I couldn't use a mask or anything because it would have been smashed against the hull – the waves were about 12 feet and it was blowing force 8.

'But it had to be done, for on the fourth day out it meant either abandon the race or repair the boat.' As simple as that. He says it as though abandoning the race was such a ludicrous idea it simply wasn't worth considering. It made me wonder how many other solo sailors would have given that alternative more weight when faced with the prospect of going over the side to make a repair in a full gale.

Colas' account of his race was far from being all deadly seriousness. He had his moments of reckless glory too. 'Something that certainly helped me to keep ahead of *Vendredi* was that two days before I finished, for the first time on the passage, the wind came slightly abeam, so I could ease sheets and let the boat hurtle down the waves at full throttle – as multihulls can when given the right winds. I actually covered 260 miles that day, and blocked my speedo at 20 knots.

'But the first week out was very rough. I was prepared for that. You know, I have sailed this boat around the world now, first as crew to Tabarly and then as the skipper. Coming round the Cape of Good Hope and across the Bay of Biscay I had plenty of bad weather – it was winter time – so I was quite ready for all the storms.'

That experience of bad weather paid off in another way. Colas realised that by making the mast and rigging stiffer he could make the boat more resistant to foul weather and at the same time increase her ability to go to windward. So when at last *Pen Duick IV* was given a refit in Brittany after completing 44,000 miles of ocean voyaging, he fitted a bigger forestay and an additional backstay attached to the main hull to augment the original ones attached to the outriggers.

'The extra rigging made a very stiff set-up, making tons and tons of compression in the mast and in the boat. But I knew the boat could stand it – and that's what enabled me to go to windward. Also Victor Tonnere, the sailmaker in Lorient, made perfect sails for me. Every day I would say to myself, "Goodness, this mainsail is drawing well," or "Goodness, my jib is taking me to Newport." I could feel it within myself, you know.'

And Colas smiled the big smile of the winner; of the man who has dedicated years of his life to one over-riding ambition and is experiencing the exultation of at last achieving that moment of glory.

Glory for the boat as well as the skipper. Colas was quick to point how well *Pen Duick* had performed. 'Look,' he said. 'This boat is a multihull and multihulls are supposed not to go to windward – good for reaching and downhill work, and that's all. But *Pen Duick* has won a windward race across the Atlantic. And it beat a 128-footer specifically designed for windward work by one of America's best architects. This is the fastest sailing boat in the world. There is a no doubt about it. It is not just that she has won this race, but all her other records. She has them all now: fastest transatlantic passage, fastest across the Indian Ocean, fastest across the Pacific, fastest day's run or week's run or month's run.'

But the other point about multihulls is that they are supposed to be better suited to the southern route. Tom Follett did very well with *Cheers* four years ago. Wasn't Colas tempted to head that way? His answer was yet another piece of evidence for the case that here was the most determined man ever to enter the Observer race. 'I never doubted that I would take the northern, great circle route. In fact, I was prepared to go much further north if necessary, but I was working from a weather facsimile machine – it produces a map of the weather pattern several times a day – so I knew where to go.

'I saw clearly that the high northern route would mean tough winds without any rewarding angle of sailing, and I could see, too, that on the southern route the wind was too light. So there was only one way to go – the shortest way. Anyway I had set my mind that I would take the shortest route feasible, start as fast as possible, accelerate all the way and sprint for the finish.'

But even such intense determination as Colas produces cannot do very much about the fitful weather that slowed most competitors down on the run-in to Newport. But that doesn't stop him trying. 'After I met Terlain I had four days of calms, which were most frustrating. But at the same time I knew that he was bound to have some calms as well and that he would go slower in them than me.

'My boat, being lighter, will go faster. And I have been through so many calms, sailing around the world, that I am sure I have more guts to get the boat out of a calm than the others have. I just sit up there at the helm – the night through if necessary – because I know I must get out. I would be prepared to row, even to sit and blow into the sails, to get away. The wind will not come to me. It is up to me to get out of the calm towards the wind.'

When I asked Colas about his future, after the great triumph, he replied, 'A lot depended upon my winning the race. I borrowed all the money to get this boat and get her ready. I have been repaying for a couple of years and still have several years to go. Perhaps winning will help me become fully her owner.

'After that, there are so many things one can do. Why not go out and get more records? There are still some that hold good since the time of the square-riggers. It would tickle me pink to do something like that.

'I shall write a book about the voyage and how I prepared for the race. Perhaps I will add another chapter on how I sail *Pen Duick* home. I don't know yet if I will go the easy way, calling at Bermuda and the Azores, with Teura, my brother, and friends, or whether I will go alone by the northern route and tackle the square-riggers' record.'

This was a man talking within a couple of hours of crossing the finishing line after a 3,000 mile singlehanded race. Already he was setting himself new targets. I could not help remembering my chat with Sir Francis Chichester after he returned to Plymouth in a battered *Gipsy Moth V* in May 1971. He had attempted many high speed runs across the Atlantic; had completed 18,000 miles alone at sea; had suffered a severe knock-down that very nearly caused him to abandon ship. Yet when I asked him if he considered going for the Observer Single-handed just over a year later his reply was, 'I like a bit of sport.' Colas showed me that same kind of insatiable drive huddled in his tiny cabin that night in Newport. Always new targets, always new challenges to his seemingly inexhaustible endeavour.

There was no doubt in my mind that night. The 1972 Observer Singlehanded race had been won by a man of great courage, skill, and willpower. Alain Colas was a worthy successor to Chichester, Tabarly, and Williams.

13   Runners-up

In one sense, there was no way that Jean-Yves Terlain could win the 1972 Observer Singlehanded. If he had sailed the big schooner across the line first, everyone would have given the credit to the enormous waterline length of *Vendredi 13*. And he started the race fully aware that if he failed, nobody would give his boat as the excuse.

So it was an even more bitter pill to swallow when he was beaten into second place by the narrow margin of 16 hours. He arrived while the euphoria of Colas' great victory still hung in the Newport air, and he learned that victory was not his only when he was one hour from the finishing line. But he had begun to be anxious about the result as early as 5 am on Saturday 8 July, because he was becalmed for hours. When eventually he did reach the Port O'Call Marina he announced sadly that he was disappointed with his own performance – he had planned to get to the finish in under 20 days. 'But,' he added, 'one cannot reproach the weather.'

Smiling despite his disappointment, and sporting a newly-grown moustache and beard, Terlain said that he had had a very safe trip along the great circle route. There was no time when he had been afraid, although he did think, during the worst of the weather, that something might break on *Vendredi 13*. In fact, nothing did. The only other yacht he saw on the whole trip was *Pen Duick IV* when it passed him. But like so many others, Terlain was not pleased by the gentle weather of the 1972 race. He needed good winds to keep the 35 tons of his big schooner moving well, and all too often they were missing. Indeed, his best day's passage was only 200 miles – 'Rather little for this boat,' he admitted. He was convinced that if he had not invested in those genoas he would still have been in mid-ocean.

The mystery of his radio was soon solved – he had never been able to start his engines. It seemed to be something to do with the angle of heel that the craft took up as soon as she was in a blow. 'I am going to have an expert prove the engines have never turned,' said Terlain. 'I am sure they are full of water or something.'

Terlain seemed quite genuine in his congratulations to Alain Colas, despite the rumours of animosity between them. '*Pen Duick IV* is a fantastic machine,' he said, 'but imagine living on it. *Vendredi* is a boat you can live in, a house you can carry on your back. We have proved that her design is a formula which is practicable, for cruising as well as racing.'

Later in the week, when Brian Cooke arrived in *British Steel*, Terlain commiserated with the British entrant about the lack of wind. 'After the first week it was suddenly summertime,' said Terlain. 'It would have been much better for us if we had had the same conditions as last time. I am sure we could increase the performance of *Vendredi* by 20 per cent at least.'

Cooke asked the Frenchman, 'How big for the next race, Jean-Yves?' and Terlain replied, 'I don't know yet. Maybe a bit bigger. It was not a question of human power problems – only of finances. She was not difficult to handle at all. There was a lot of movement in the cockpit at the back. The idea of that was to keep the whole deck area clear for work. But maybe it would be better to have a cockpit in the middle, even if it is under a boom or whatever.'

There must have been a lot of movement in the ends. When I went below on *Vendredi* I was intrigued to see that the famous silver crash helmet had also served its purpose by preventing Terlain's head cracking against the cabin top when a whip in the great length of the schooner shot him skyward like a springboard. The silver surface was chipped and dented in many places.

But in the right conditions *Vendredi 13* obviously whooshed along magnificently. 'As soon as you have winds from the side, it's just smooth,' said her skipper. 'Sometimes you wake up and think "What's happening? I've stopped. It's not moving at all." Then you look at the speedometer and she's doing 7, 8, or 9 knots.' Terlain's was a brave, if costly, effort to win the 1972 race. And every competitor in every future race will learn something from his gallant failure.

Both *Pen Duick IV* and *Vendredi 13* crossed the Atlantic by the great circle route. But just as in 1968, when Tom Follett crept in with *Cheers* from the

Azores route, so in 1972 Jean-Marie Vidal took third place by coming up from the south. That gave France a devastating one-two-three, and unarguably established that the trimaran victory was no fluke, for here was a 53-foot tri beating home several big monohulls with more length in the water.

Vidal's appearance at the finishing line actually took quite a few of us by surprise. We heard from him early on the morning of 11 July and knew that he estimated his arrival at about 5 pm But his watch was still set to Plymouth time, and he actually crossed the line soon after noon, American time on the east coast. I was half way through an hour-long radio broadcast from Christie's, the local seafood restaurant, when *The Observer*'s promotions manager, Elizabeth Balcon, came in and scribbled a note about *Cap 33*'s finishing time. This meant that the listeners to station WKFD were among the first to know that Vidal had taken third place. Even Vidal's wife, who was waiting in Newport to greet him, was caught out by his sudden appearance. Friends had to comb the town looking for her as the sleek yellow multihull came up to the quay.

No sooner was Vidal secured than Alain Colas leapt aboard and the two started an animated discussion about the technical aspects of their relative performances. Thirty-year-old Vidal, bronzed and fit, had obviously enjoyed his race – or 'cruise' as he often called it. But he was still somewhat disappointed not to have made a faster time. 'My boat is too heavy,' he told Joanna Kilmartin, 'and I never had enough wind. She is heavy because she was designed to be strong.'

He thought Alain Colas had the vital edge over Terlain and himself because of having much greater familiarity with his craft. 'Alain had lived aboard his boat for three years and sailed 36,000 miles. Jean-Yves and I had hardly any chance to get to know our boats at all.'

Vidal's problems were few. He tore both his major foresails at the clew ring soon after leaving Plymouth and spent many hours repairing them – 'I did a better job than my sailmaker,' he said. Then he heard a mysterious noise below – mystifying enough for him to ask for guidance by radio from designer André Allegre. But before the answer came he had discovered for himself that a bolt holding the crossbeam to the main hull was working loose and needed tightening.

The self-steering on *Cap 33* was never really satisfactory. Either the mizzen sail deflected the wind from it, causing a change of course, or it was not functioning because of the breaking of the servo blade. However, Vidal was not too concerned, because the trimaran would balance herself when going to windward, and whenever there were following winds he was so intent upon making the most of them that he stayed at the helm all the time anyway.

At the end of his race, the young Frenchman admitted that the last thing he felt like doing was returning to his chemist's shop in Montpelier. But after a few days in Newport he managed to sell *Cap 33* to an American friend of Phil Weld's who had heard the multihull gospel, and back he went to central France.

My lasting memory of Jean-Marie Vidal will be of his polite refusal of Jim Morris's offer of a can of beer. 'I have plenty aboard,' he said with a smile, and we both remembered suddenly that of course he was sponsored by a brewery. But when I asked if he had drunk much beer on the way over, he said no. 'Not even wine?' I asked. 'No. Those of us who come from the Midi don't drink much alcohol,' he said.

The British supporters had been hoping that Brian Cooke and *British Steel* might beat one of the Frenchmen to a place in the first three, but in the weather that prevailed during July he had little chance to get his 59 foot ketch going hard on the wind. In the early stages, of course, he was well up with the leaders, because the fierce blows of the first week suited his solidly built craft perfectly. But when the wind eased she could not keep up with the big multihulls and the huge schooner.

Nevertheless, Cooke finished less than a day behind *Cap 33* in a creditable time of 24 days, 19 hours, and 28 minutes, and since that was still much faster than Geoffrey Williams' winning time in 1968, he did have the consolation of knowing that he was the fastest British solo sailor across the Atlantic.

Always unassuming, Brian Cooke seemed quite surprised to find that so many people were up to greet him when *British Steel* came alongside at Port O'Call at four in the morning. He blushingly acknowledged their greetings and sipped the celebratory champagne with somewhat tentative enthusiasm.

He told me then that *British Steel* had suffered but two problems with equipment during the passage. The first was the collapse of a vital shroud on the mainmast when he was eight days out of Plymouth. The second was some bending of the stanchions on the starboard side of the deck caused by the US Coast Guard cutter which came alongside after he had crossed the line at 2.28 am on 12 July, to tow *British Steel* the rest of the way into Newport.

The Coast Guards made amends next day at the dockside. Cooke's own repairs of the earlier problem were not so easy. The broken shroud was discovered just after a gale had passed through and left little wind but an oily sea with a heavy swell. 'That was my big problem,' he said. 'It's a bit difficult coming out of a gale – when you are very, very tired – and trying to think what's the best thing to do with what you have on board. I was talking to myself aloud to make myself believe that what I was going to do was the right thing. It was a bit of a hairy operation at the time.'

That's a typical Cooke understatement. This particular hairy operation involved climbing 30 feet up the mainmast of *British Steel* during a black night, trying to work on the repair with one hand while hanging on to the viciously swinging mast with the other. Cooke went up and down that mast five times during the night to fit a wire strop around the mainmast at the spreaders in a figure of eight and fix a jury shroud to that. 'It's only hand tight,' he explained. 'It's a preventer rather than something that will do any work. I've been worried every time I was on starboard tack.'

'Surely you were tempted to leave the whole thing until daylight?' I asked. 'Yes, but I wasn't going to give away what I thought was a reasonable position at the time by losing six or eight hours. It might have been throwing away the race, or the chance of a place. Certainly it would have been throwing away all the preparation that had gone into the operation before the race.'

Next morning we looked at the repair together. He was obviously proud of the fact that when he radioed back for guidance about the best way to solve the problem and explained what he had done, the experts' answer was that his own solution could not be bettered. But the memory of the effort it had cost was still fresh.

'You can't imagine what it was like. It would be all right up there if the boat were lying still like now, but swaying from side to side was quite another thing. You know, I got a pin through the mast and had to put a split pin through the other end to hold it. There I was with this little pin in my mouth thirty feet up and swaying like anything. Do you think I could get that pin in? I just couldn't. Then when I did get it through it splayed in the wrong direction and I had to climb down for some pliers and go up to put it straight again. It's the sort of silly little job that would take five minutes here, but takes five hours at sea.'

Cooke was delighted with the performance of *British Steel*. 'She's a wonderful boat – beautifully balanced,' he said. 'But there was just not enough wind. The strongest we experienced was bordering on Force 9 just before Cape Race, about half way across. I just pushed it along as best I could. It's a heavy boat and needs a lot of wind.'

Cooke actually found enough wind to get *British Steel* across 150 miles of sea each day, but because he had head winds all the way until he reached Cape Race, he could only record about 120 miles a day made good, on average. 'Three days we were up in the 180s, but one day we only covered 80-something – that was abyssmal,' he said.

The enthusiasm of both Cooke and his craft for really strong blows came out clearly in his description of that short spell of Force 9 half way through the passage. 'We were on a reach and just tramping along in grand style,' he said, with eyes aglow and a broad smile.

Obviously it was a happy combination of yacht and yachtsman. 'I thoroughly enjoyed the passage. Of course, you have your good moments and your bad – the bad ones are not very enjoyable. But it was an easier trip than in *Opus* in 1968. This boat is well fitted up with winches and gear. I didn't find handling her much of a physical problem. And as a sail she is much less tiring than a smaller boat. The movement was very easy. Quite a lot of times I was doing 5 or 6 knots with hardly any motion at all. An easier ride, and a quicker one too.'

As the time elapsed since the start of the race at Plymouth exceeded the 25 days and 20 hours taken by *Sir Thomas Lipton* in 1968, we began to wonder what had become of Tom Follett. Four years earlier he had sailed *Cheers* into Newport in 27 days. Surely the new trimaran *Three Cheers* was a faster boat?

There was a growing concern to be read in the faces of the usually ever-cheerful Project Cheers team – backer Jim Morris and designer Dick Newick were in Newport with their families and Tom's wife Priscilla, all waiting the arrival of the bright yellow boat.

Most of us were probably thinking about the uncluttered lines of the trimaran as we had seen her in Plymouth – uncluttered by guard rails – and remembering Tom Follett's disinclination to use a safety harness.

As the week drew on a heavy sea fog descended on Narragansett Bay, and it seemed to echo the vague fear that something disastrous could have happened to one of the most-liked of solo sailors. But Col. Odling-Smee refused to worry unnecessarily. 'He's just found a hole in the wind,' he told me.

And he was right. On Friday evening, just when the participants and pressmen had begun to cast care aside at an informal party in a nearby restaurant-cum-bar with the slightly odd title of the Candy Store, the word swept through the place that 'Tom's arrived!'

He had not been seen by the Coast Guard. He had not been met at the line. Suddenly he was there, looming yellow out of the fog at the end of the Port O'Call jetty. The unexpectedness of his arrival made the relief at seeing that unmistakable shape all the more intense. Follett himself looked happy and well, wearing a crumpled canvas hat that had as many creases in it as his weather-worn face.

His time for the passage was 27 days, 11 hours, 4 minutes – a few hours longer than he had taken in *Cheers*. He was disappointed with the performance because *Three Cheers* is potentially much faster than the proa, but he had suffered badly from lack of winds.

'I went further north than last time, but I guess I should have gone south,' he said when he arrived. 'I just had very bad winds. I kept looking for some and didn't get any – except the first week and a half and then I got too much. The wind would blow enough to kick up a sea then die off to a flat calm again.'

Follett always takes the absolute minimum of stores on a transatlantic voyage. This time he almost overdid it. 'I drank my last can of beer two days ago, but I still have one gallon left of the five

gallons of water I took. I have two cans of soup and one can of carrots, and a few crackers. I had to get in today or I would have starved to death,' he said with a laugh.

He found it difficult to understand the increasing concern of the Project Cheers team. 'Getting worried about me?' he asked incredulously. 'How come?'

When I asked him if he now stood by his estimate made before the race that given the right conditions *Three Cheers* could get to America in 16 days, Follett replied, 'Sure, I could take ten days off this time. But I had one day this trip of only 31 miles and lots of days of 60, 70, 80 – that sort of thing. I was pretty discouraged. I did have one really good day when I thought, "By George, this is the day I am going to make 300 miles." But when it ended I was down to bare poles. I think that was the day that *Second Life* lost its mast. I ended up covering just 180 miles that day.'

Alain Colas was there to see the American in. He said, 'When I saw how your boat was sailing on the first afternoon, I thought to myself – and I wrote in my log – "The race is between Jean-Yves, Tom, and me." I was much worried.'

'Yeah. I thought so too,' replied Follett laconically.

As the first American home, Follett took for the second time the special trophy given by the Ida Lewis Yacht Club of Newport.

Gerard Pestey sprung the surprise of the race by following *Three Cheers* over the line in his 55 foot cruising trimaran *Architeuthis*, just 51 minutes later. He completed the passage in 27 days, 11 hours, 55 minutes, but was subject to a 24 hour penalty for not arriving in Plymouth by the check-in deadline the week before the race.

The tough little Frenchman made a diplomatic speech to the waiting crowd about how pleased he was to be in America for the first time – perhaps because he knew he had not obtained a proper visa for his visit. The US Customs authorities were understanding and gave him a temporary seaman's visiting permit.

He, too, suffered from light winds, but had more success than Follett, following a far southerly course between the Azores and the trade wind routes, and actually totting up 269 miles on one day. He had trouble finding the Brenton Reef tower to finish, an experience shared by Follett, who said, 'There's such a fog out there you can't see two feet in front of you. I homed in on the tower by the bleepers (radio direction finding beacons) and I almost hit the thing before I could see it.'

By this time, of course, Bill Howell was in Newport after his crippled catamaran had been towed in. He it was who dissolved the emotional tension at Tom Follett's arrival by catching sight of the glisten in Dick Newick's eye and calling out good-naturedly 'Now stop crying – he's all right!' And to Priscilla Follett, also near to tears, the Australian twang boomed, 'You didn't think you'd got rid of him, did yer?'

Howell had good cause to be cheerful, even if his own boat had suffered. The multihulls he believed in so much had swept the board, taking first, third, fifth, and sixth places – and but for that Russian trawler would have taken the seventh spot too.

That fell to the second Englishman home, Martin Minter-Kemp sailing the big cutter *Strongbow*. He arrived on the evening of Saturday 15 July, just too late to place ahead of *Architeuthis* because of the latter's 24-hour penalty. We had heard that *Strongbow* had more than her share of problems on the way over, but Minter-Kemp looked serene and rested. Indeed, I couldn't help thinking what a sharp contrast these 1972 finishers made to the pictures on the wall in Peter Dunning's office which showed Geoffrey Williams, Bruce Dalling, and Bill Howell at the end of their 1968 races, red-eyed and weary.

Strongbow had sailed into head winds for all but 29 hours of her 28½ day crossing, and had survived two knockdowns. As Martin Minter-Kemp related the story of his voyage, it became apparent that he had experienced one of the most gruelling passages of all the 1972 contestants.

'Of the two knockdowns, the first was very bad for morale, as I had only just started, and the second stove in a bulkhead in the forward cabin,' he said. Had he felt like giving up when his morale was low? 'I certainly did at that stage. She was leaking, and I don't like a boat that leaks, but I plugged the leaks – hammered them down with copper tacks – and carried on. Then, towards the end of the trip my steering gear was a problem. The generator flew off the stern like a catherine wheel in the night, during a gale, and after that my auto pilot was a

white elephant. I had to stay at the wheel 18 hours a day for the last 2,000 miles.'

How did he manage for sleep, then? 'I slept an hour or so at a time, for maybe four or five hours a day. I slept during calms and when we were hard on the wind and *Strongbow* would balance herself. I also found I could sleep at the helm. I could feel when the wind went round onto the other cheek and actually give the wheel a kick with my foot and carry on sleeping. It seemed to work.

'I got off to a bad start. From the gun the wind freshened from the southwest – the wrong direction – and there was a heavy ground swell. In fact, the wind was in an unfavourable direction until the first week was over. That first night I suppose I was still in a state of euphoria after the start. Anyway, we had this knockdown between Land's End and the Scillies. I damaged my knee, the crash broke all the battens in the mainsail, and there was some minor damage to the rigging. There was also a slight but persistent leak where the skin was flexing near the forward cabin and the laminates had started to weep. However, I put all those things right the next day and carried on.

'*Strongbow* took a continual pounding going to windward. But then, that's what she was built for. One either had to move or not. I could pay off and go 50 degrees to the wind and the pounding would stop, but that's no good. She should be 38 to 40 degrees to the wind and making 7 or 8 knots close hauled. It's punishing for the boat, but I had my orders from the designer and builder to drive her hard, and that's what I did.'

But wasn't he carrying too much sail that first night, to suffer a knockdown like that? 'Yes, I probably was. You see, there was a great mass of boats trying to get clear. I was cracking on, enjoying a personal duel with Gerard Dijkstra in *Second Life* – we were tacking through each other to compare speeds. I was carrying a big heavy yankee, a staysail, and main fully reefed. I carried on like that until I lost *Second Life*.

'Then when night fell it blew up quickly and I hung on too long. I should have reduced, there's no question. Had it happened a week out I would have been attuned to the need to reduce sail. Luckily, the damage was more to my self-confidence than anything else. The rest was just minor damage. But the continuous pounding was a different matter. I was either going to race to America or not, so I just had to put up with a great crash about every fourth sea.'

Now there are really no bilges aboard *Strongbow*. One stands virtually on the hull of the boat. I wondered, if it was necessary to pump the boat whenever she was on port tack and those sprung laminations were letting in water, what she was like to live in below. 'Well, the forward cabin was meant to be my hidey-hole where it would be warm, dry, and cosy. But after that it was anything but warm, dry, or cosy. I spent the rest of the trip in the centre passage where the raised floor was above the level of the water – in about six square feet, in fact.

'The second knockdown came on 1 July, after I had spoken with Chris Brasher at *The Observer* through the *QE2*. I was in a marvellous state of optimism because Chris had said that he thought only *British Steel* and one other – *Pen Duick*, I think – were ahead of me. And the *QE2* people had been so kind to me. You know I asked them to confirm my position, and they said did I want it from exactly where I was or to the nearest 100 feet! Their instruments are so good that they can give a different position for each end of the ship!

'That night we had the storm. *Second Life*, who was only about 100 miles away from me, lost her mast. This time I reduced sail in good time. At 30 knots of wind I was down to mainsail and staysail; at 35 knots, staysail only. At 40 knots *Strongbow* fell out of a wave for about 16 feet through what I describe as a hole in the water. There was a bloody great crash below, so I took the staysail down and went to see what it was. The starboard forward bulkhead had collapsed and been driven inwards about three inches. The planks had started and the leak was now worse. By this time it was registering a steady 45 knots on the anemometer, probably gusting up to 50 knots.

'Yet the next morning, only 12 hours later, I had the genoa up; but it was from that position, about 42 degrees west, that I had to sail myself.'

How did he feel about finishing seventh for the second time? 'Disappointed, of course. Very sad. If I had had a proper working up time things might have been different. I think she could win it next time. But you see I didn't get her until June. I did the qualifying cruise with just two sails, no steering gear, and some of the guardrail still missing. I only had 12 days' sailing with her before the race started. We got her to Plymouth and just went on building her. I reckon she was complete about 20 minutes before the start.'

So if another four years would make all the difference, how did Minter-Kemp feel about sailing her himself next time? 'Well, you know, I'm afraid I am still multihull minded. For this race I lobbied for an 83 foot trimaran – I had a model built and everything. She would have been very fast, but public opinion was against a multihull after the '68 race.'

Strongbow left Newport without Minter-Kemp. Skippered by Paul Weychan, and with a full crew, she set out to establish a new record time from Brenton Reef to Plymouth breakwater with a challenge from David Dorman, representing her sponsors Bulmer's Cider, to any other yacht that wished to have a 'fun' race downhill to England with full crew aboard.

Dorman offered a Bulmer's trophy for the competition. Bill Howell's response was characteristically sharp: 'Then the multihulls will beat you by an even bigger margin.'

14 French style

As if taking the first three places in the race were not enough, France also mopped up the under 35-foot trophy and the special Royal Western award for the first woman home. It was a fair reflection of the way the French singlehanders had dominated the race, for out of their 13 original starters, 10 finished inside the first 20 – a remarkable demonstration of their skill and determination to win.

After the triumph of the first trio of winners, the most impressive exploit was undoubtedly Alain Gliksman's eighth position in the tiny *Toucan*. She is just under 35 foot in length and just over 6 foot beam yet he brought her across the ocean in 28½ days, finishing a mere ten minutes behind the 65-foot *Strongbow*. That was more than three days ahead of the next yacht under 35 foot (Mike McMullen's *Binkie II*) and fast enough to have taken fourth place in the 1968 race ahead of such powerful machines as *Spirit of Cutty Sark*, *Gancia Girl*, and *Myth of Malham*.

Although he was so close to Martin Minter-Kemp at the finish, Gliksman appeared at Port O'Call much later. Because of the fog around the Narragansett Bay, he did not attempt to get in on Saturday night, but sailed calmly in at first light on Sunday morning, tied up at the end of the dock and modestly went to sleep. We found him there in the morning, still bleary-eyed from the first decent rest he had had in four weeks.

When he began to talk about the sort of trip he had experienced, it was not difficult to see why he needed to catch up. 'This is the wettest boat I have ever had,' he told me. 'The hull is designed for speed with no other consideration. There is no flair so there is nothing to deflect the water. That's why I found my crash helmet and plastic visor so useful. When the wind is about force 5 or 6 you cannot look to windward – you feel as though you are under a fireman's hose – though it is salt water. Well this boat does about seven knots to windward, it really moves under any jib – changing sail doesn't make a lot of difference to it. I found her so fast that I had to slow her down before I broke her.

'Of course, this means you get spray in the face all the time, and the visor is very good for that. I'm going to stick to it on every boat. Whatever you are sailing you have to be in an exposed position to see where you are going and after a while are just blind. This is the answer.

'And the boat was uncomfortable in other ways. It is not a problem of size below. The berth is quite big and there is plenty of room, except when you want to put your trousers on. But when you are going to windward in anything above 5 or 6 she shakes in every direction and the noise level is very high, so you cannot sleep. You see, the hull is built under tension so it's like being inside a guitar. You just have to lie there and wait because you cannot sleep. And after two days like that all your body is painful and really crying out for rest. Yet no matter how exhausted you are you cannot sleep.'

Gliksman spoke in a very straightforward manner, with no false heroics about his experience. But it was easy to see that the voyage had made its mark on his mind and body. The eyes, always dark and penetrating, now had the fierce, sharp look of the deeply weary. The body, never indulged, now looked spare and wiry. With the wild mane of black hair and ample beard, he looked like some modern-day Robinson Crusoe just returned to civilisation.

But why had he chosen such a punishing boat? When he began to outline his reasons, all the purpose and will of the French faction seemed to come to the surface. 'After the last race I came back to the designer of *Raph*, André Mauric, and said I needed a boat with much more sail area to wetted surface, because the problem was keeping going in light airs. Also I didn't want a boat that was stiff like *Raph*, but one with a flat stability curve so that it would allow some latitude in the use of varying sail plans in different weather conditions, because a singlehander cannot always be changing sail to match the wind.

'This meant a narrow boat, and the good thing with a narrow boat is that if you make it heel that doesn't destroy the line like it does with a beamy boat. I don't like the modern IOR boats because when they heel it is like trying to drown a cat – it keeps wanting to come up again; it gets wild and you are getting nowhere. But a long and narrow boat keeps going.

'So we designed a boat – in fact, it was a bit like *Strongbow* – but I could not finance it. So I had no boat, but I was aware of this design being built in Switzerland as an open yacht for lake racing – rather like a 5·5 metre. Up in Lac Léman they have very wide experience of racing boat against boat, you know. And *Toucan*'s design was doing very well there. Of course, by sea standards it was very small, but the thing was – I could afford it. So I bought the hull and got the builder to put a cabin on it. My hope was that it would be fast enough to go south and find the decent weather, and still save its time.'

'As *Cheers* did in 1968?' I asked. 'Yes. In a way, the whole project was inspired by the *Cheers* story. I thought if a man could live in *Cheers* he could live in *Toucan*. The only trouble is that I'm not as good as Tom Follett at dropping equipment – I still carry too much.

'Due to the bad weather at the start I kept going south. I didn't actually want to go round the Azores but as the wind was still westerly I had no choice. I went south of the main islands of Terceira and Fayal. Then I kept going west – doing about 180 miles a day along the 38th parallel. I wanted to keep doing that and wait for a good south-westerly to take me up across the Gulf Stream, but the south-westerlies came early and pushed me further and further north from about 50 degrees west until the finish.

'Eventually I had to come back down from Nantucket to the finishing line. I think I lost a lot of time in the Gulf Stream. One day I was worried about going so far north and turned south again. For a day and a night I went that way, but then I was becalmed for a whole day, so when the wind came again I turned north once more.

'If I had had more detailed knowledge of where the centre of the anticyclone was I might have stayed south of it, but I couldn't carry a weather machine like the big boats and I could get very little information from the radio, so I just had to go with the wind. Anything rather than get caught in calms. Of course, the Gulf Stream isn't comfortable. The weather builds up very quickly and you get short seas which stop you completely.

'When the first two boats were home – on 7 July – I had 700 miles to go and could have done it in 3½

days with decent weather. That would have got me to Newport in 23 days. But that was when the trouble began. Those last 700 miles took me 8½ days. This crossing was much slower than last time.'

For all that, Gliksman actually reached the Azores in 11 days and up to the 18th day of his passage he never covered less than 140 miles in the day. Then he became stuck in the Gulf Stream for three days.

Toucan is certainly a remarkable little boat. With her slim shape and bendy mast she reminds one of a singlehanded dinghy rather than an ocean-going racer. Her skipper reckons that she will do 15 knots with the wind on the beam and spoke proudly of overtaking a class 1 IOR racer that was flying a spinnaker, while *Toucan* had a very modest sail plan, during a race in the Mediterranean that involved a dead run. But there was no dead run for Gliksman on the way to Newport. He was close-hauled virtually all the time and managed to get the spinnaker up only twice.

Toucan's capture of the trophy for boats up to 35 foot overall was really a triumph of good planning and sound seamanship. It has set a standard for the new award which will be difficult to match. Similarly, the way Marie-Claude Fauroux swept up the winning lady's title was dauntingly methodical, and one wonders how long her record for the crossing – 32 days, 22 hours, and one minute – will stand before it is broken.

Half past eight in the morning is not exactly the most romantic hour of the day, but that certainly did not inhibit the meeting between Marie-Claude and Yves-Louis Pinaud on the dockside at the Port O'Call Marina just after she arrived as fourteenth finisher on the morning of 14 July, easily the first of the three women singlehanders in the race. He had just given her a necklet as a symbol of their intention to marry.

Pinaud is the ex-Finn and Flying Dutchman champion of France who helped Marie-Claude Fauroux prepare for her entry in the 1972 race, but the first woman home had no idea that he was in America until I told her. Her eyes lit up and she wanted to know why he wasn't there to greet her. It did not take long for him to appear – the news of a new arrival – especially one as attractive as Marie-Claude – travels fast in Newport.

Whether she expected to see Pinaud or not, Mademoiselle Fauroux was well turned out to meet the welcomers at the dockside. Her 35-foot sloop *Aloa VII* looked trim and well-maintained, while the skipper was immaculate in striped jeans and pink sweater, her long hair neatly plaited and her teeth shining white as she smiled shyly to the well-wishers.

Marie-Claude had expected to cross the line on the Monday evening or Tuesday morning, but, like so many others, the last part of her voyage had been dogged by calms and fogs. She had in fact lost most of three days completing the last leg from the Nantucket Light Vessel to Newport. 'I heard cargo boats going by and lots of sirens,' she said. 'When you are sitting there in the fog with no wind and all those fog horns, it's very disturbing. I was constantly worried about being run down.'

She was very happy to know that she had won the trophy for the first woman home but there was no gloating over her defeat of Yves Olivaux in *Aloa I*, a boat virtually identical to her own. She had heard the reports on the radio about Olivaux's suspected broken arm soon after the start and was quick to acknowledge that this would obviously affect his performance.

Although she said she needed plenty of heating from the stove on *Aloa VII* at the start of the race – perhaps not surprising from one used to the kindly climate of Cannes – she made her best daily mileages up to half way across. Then she was covering at least 110 miles a day, but when she approached the American seaboard she was often down to 40 miles a day at the most.

The boat performed perfectly, she said, and her self-steering gear was 'formidable'. When I said that she seemed very calm and relaxed, she replied simply, 'That is because I have had no problems.' She ate well, but drank very little wine – only two litres on the whole voyage. But she did not enjoy cooking for herself – 'the constant rolling of a boat as small as this in the Atlantic swells makes cooking a bit of a problem'.

Despite being penalised 50 minutes for being over the line at the start – a sign, perhaps, of her background as a Moth dinghy sailor, and champion – Marie-Claude Fauroux kept her fourteenth place. The next boat home – Jock Brazier's *Flying Angel* – was nearly nine hours behind her.

She told the waiting reporters – translation kindly provided by Gerard Pestey, because Marie-Claude's English is minimal – that this would be her first and last transatlantic race. 'Once is enough. I wanted to do it to prove I could, but I don't see what it would prove to go again.'

But was she never afraid, someone asked? 'Yes, I was very scared when I saw the SS *France*, the luxury liner, looming by quite close to starboard. It was difficult to tell how close it was, but it seemed very big and I felt very small,' she said. Her course had been the same kind of odd mixture of Azores and rhumb-line route that Follett and Gliksman had followed. She passed just north of the islands and then headed more or less directly for Nantucket. It was the kind of simple answer to the problem that you might expect from someone as direct and determined as Marie-Claude. Almost as though she were defying the Gulf Stream to set her back.

But whether she was affected by the Gulf Stream or no, she certainly sailed the boat hard all the way. Again it is interesting to compare her time with those put up four years earlier. With a 33-day passage she would have come sixth then, or fourth in the 1964 race. A truly remarkable performance for a 26-year-old girl. And one that fully deserves to be rewarded with a special trophy.

15   *They Also Sailed*

As my all too short stay in Newport neared its end, I became more and more aware of the fact that no solo sailor who reaches Newport ever actually loses the Observer Singlehanded race. All those who successfully negotiate 3,000 and more miles of North Atlantic have certainly won a major competition. They have proved the seaworthiness of their boats, they have demonstrated the efficiency of their navigation, above all they have proved their own seamanship. No matter that in those crucial weeks of June, July, and August 1972 the North Atlantic proved to be less ferocious than it might have been – its challenge is always a daunting one, and all who meet it successfully should take their rightful credit for winning through.

Take the case of the quiet American, Jim Ferris. He sailed his Morgan 54 *Whisper* over the line at Brenton Tower in the evening of 16 July. It was dark and there was the inevitable fog about, so he thought it more seamanlike to wait for the clearer conditions of the morning. And at first light he was seen sitting serenely aboard the boat at the end of the Port O'Call jetty, calmly sidestepping any questions about dramas on his passage. Well yes, he had had to call into the Azores because a running backstay had broken, but he only lost six hours and once that was repaired he had had a good run. Yes, he found the swivel chair in front of his steering wheel quite useful at sea because he had spent many hours at the helm. No, he didn't feel too tired.

One had to read between the lines of this ultra-modest script to realise that Ferris had sailed his boat very hard for Newport. To have completed the journey in under 30 days, including an involuntary stop, was an achievement that many a solo sailor would envy, yet Jim made little of it and soon faded away to his home not far away in Massachusetts, shunning the public attention of any of the numerous parties in Newport.

Franco Faggioni came in a day before Jim Ferris. We heard that he was not far away after he had crossed the line and was being towed in by a helpful couple out motor-boating in the bay. So we went out to relieve the tow and bring the smiling Italian

to harbour. He turned out to be better at smiling than at exaggerating the rigours of his crossing, for the only thing he was prepared to grumble about was the frailty of the wind. One might have expected some complaint about the lack of headroom aboard *Sagittario*, for Franco's bald pate bore witness to the fact that it had recently been in sharp contact with some part of the boat. But he smiled and made friends and produced raffia-clad bottles of Italian wine, and kept his peace.

The arrival of Chris Baranowski in Newport gained a special significance. For one thing, he was the first man from behind the Iron Curtain ever to complete the course in an Observer Singlehanded race; second, he sailed into a part of the New England coast which is the home of a large number of families descended from Polish imigrants. So when *Polonez* came up to the quay on the morning of 18 July – she crossed the line just before midnight on the 17th – there was a particularly effusive welcome for him.

Baranowski had hoped to finish higher than 12th. As his beautifully-made yacht was strongly constructed to combat high winds and rough seas, he had been looking for much tougher conditions than he found along the northern route. He actually suffered three days of almost complete calm off Newfoundland near the end of his trip. His other frustration was the loss of 12 valuable hours when he found the chainplates on *Polonez* working loose. He thought this was the result of the knockdown he suffered in the English Channel when on the way to Plymouth for the start of the race. The job involved removing a fuel tank, then putting fresh bolts through the chainplates, so it must have been quite a sweat to get it completed even in 12 hours.

That *Polonez* was prepared for anything the North Atlantic might throw at her quickly became apparent when I went aboard at Newport. In the sail locker were no less than 20 different sails. 'I used mainly the light weather ones,' said Baranowski. 'The strongest wind force I ever logged was force 8. I was tacking all the time like crazy.'

Like so many others, Baranowski found the last

part of the voyage the most tedious and the most dangerous. 'I felt sorry about it, because I really crossed the ocean in 17 days,' he said. 'The rest of the 31 days were used up getting past Newfoundland, Nova Scotia, and the Gulf of Maine. I didn't expect to sail the whole of the last week in fog. The last night of the passage was the worst of the lot. There was no wind, but strong currents – I was just going from one foghorn to the next, and one tidal race to the other.'

Still, the Pole quickly cast off the tedium of those last few hours and was soon welcoming a never-ending flow of visitors, many of them speaking to him in Polish with a distinctly American accent. They were all asked into his comfortable cabin, given some real Polish vodka and a *Polonez* badge (specially made by the Polish Yachting Association which sponsored Baranowski's entry). Then he would sit in the cockpit in the warmth of the Newport evening and sing Polish folk songs to a lute – a disarmingly charming ambassador who melted the resistance of many a chary American educated to believe that any-one from a Communist country must automatically be a double-dyed villain.

When Gliksman sailed *Toucan* into Newport, the French had taken five of the first eight places. It was a ratio they could not possibly maintain, but they did keep a 50-50 balance going until the first score of boats were home. It was Marc Linski who kept the numbers even in the first dozen by sailing *Isles du Frioul* into 11th place, notwithstanding his 75-minute penalty for being so eager to get going at the start. As the unpainted hull was tied up alongside *British Steel* at Newport, we wondered if we would now have the final showdown about that luffing match with Terlain a month earlier. Linski's pulpit was a distinctly odd shape and the word went around that he had rammed *Vendredi 13* when his patience finally expired.

But Colonel Odling-Smee was not inviting any unpleasant decisions. He did not mention a protest to Linski, and the Frenchman did not raise the matter. Then within a couple of days he and Jean-Yves Terlain were seen with their arms cordially round each other and there was a communal sigh of relief. It did seem all a long time ago, and both sailors must have realised that a dispute at that stage would make very little difference to either of their fortunes in the race. So the matter was dropped.

It turned out that Linski had been hit by the fierce gale of the night of 30 June/1 July – and 'hit' is the appropriate word, for it blew out the yacht's light weather genoa, smashed the self-steering, and threw the skipper across the boat so that he crashed his right hand into uselessness. 'After, it was not very good,' he said in his halting English. 'I was going fairly slowly. I spoke to Radio St Pierre and the doctor told me to put my hand into a splint because it sounded as though I had broken the wrist. I had a lot of pain and could not get very much sleep. Deep inside me now I am very, very tired.'

Hardly surprising when you consider that Linski had actually sailed the last 1,400 miles of his passage with only his left hand functioning, no self-steering, and almost continuous pain. It was a courageous sail and well worth his position inside the first dozen finishers.

Another Frenchman who arrived later the same week had also sailed most of the way with only one hand fit for action. This was Yves Olivaux, who brought the second Aloa to the finish line early on 22 July, in 17th place. The 62-year-old ex-jet pilot had become the oldest competitor in the race when Sir Francis Chichester pulled out, but he certainly showed some of the younger men that there was plenty of fight in him, for though he suspected he had broken both wrist and elbow in a fall on deck just four days after the start, he decided to push on to the finish.

A month later, having finally reached Newport, he was still saving the arm whenever possible, and told me that it was very sore and partially paralysed. Proper medical attention in Newport revealed that Linski's trouble was a severely ripped tendon, while Olivaux seemed to have strained his wrist badly and chipped his elbow. For them both it really was a singlehanded race.

But lest it might seem that this stage of the race was one long procession of French boats, I must report the riotous arrival of Mike McCullen in *Binkie II*. He was hulloa-ing happily and swigging champagne with abandon before the fenders were even over the side. Just under 32 days alone at sea had done nothing to dim the effervescence of this joyful Marine captain. He had a party going, with every kind of drink on tap, within a few minutes of tying up at the dock – and that was at nine o'clock in the morning!

Binkie II took 13th place, and for a long time seemed set to win the monohull handicap trophy as well. She had made very good time along the northern route, even though her skipper found the calms and fogs 'bloody frustrating'. He had a most exciting passage just before he crossed the line in the thick fog that lay over the approaches to Newport. 'I sailed between Martha's Vineyard and Noman's Land, and I didn't see either of them,' he said with a nervous kind of laugh. 'All I saw was the number five buoy. I simply sailed through on echo-soundings and DF.' Bill Muessel, the local Coast Guard Chief Bosun and authority on Narragansett Bay, looked somewhat glum. 'I wouldn't boast about that too much around here if I were you, Mike,' he said.

But for all his seeming to laugh at any kind of peril – perhaps a natural accompaniment to life in a man whose career is keyed to perilous situations – McMullen had a very real appreciation of the most dangerous moments of his trip. He was perfectly frank about his fear when among the icebergs, and he did not hesitate to say how he had felt when he thought he was going to be run down in the fog near Brenton Tower. 'I was so nearly run down,' he said. 'I've no clue what it was. It just had this bloody great horn and it seemed very close indeed. I was so frightened.'

The only equipment problem aboard *Binkie II* had been a broken forestay. The fitting on the deck simply broke in a force 7 blow. Fortunately McMullen did not have his mainsail up at the time. 'That took a few hours to repair, but other than that I had no trouble. The boat went very well. But then she's a super boat,' he said. And then he smiled and offered somebody else a drink, and soon the guitar was out and he was delighting all about him with 'The Single Girls of Singapore'. Mike McMullen is certainly in the best traditions of the 'laughing fellow-rover'.

Jock Brazier's *Flying Angel*, which took 15th place when it sailed in on 20 July, also performed very well, even though she was one of those yachts which were still being built right up to the off. Brazier had completed his qualifying cruise with the space below deck a mere shell, and *Flying Angel* was certainly the centre of much industry by Royal Engineers while she lay in Millbay Dock. In the race she gave little trouble, apart from some leaking at the chainplates.

Brazier said that he had gone particularly well until 30 March, and then he heard on the radio that both *British Steel* and *Strongbow* were going to the north. He thought that if he were to have any chance of springing a surprise among the British boats he must play a hunch – to turn south in the hope that the big boys would run into trouble and he might find better weather. So he headed down towards the line that Tom Follett was following for the first few days in July. But like so many others he found very little wind at that time and had to turn north again. His worst moment had come on 25 June when the wind suddenly shot up from force 6 to force 9 in two minutes flat. 'It was a job to get the main down,' he told me. 'All my battens were broken. But it only lasted half an hour. Nevertheless, for the next four or five hours the wind was at force 7 and the sea was such a mess that I lay ahull.'

On 7 July Brazier spotted two sailing boats not far away, both flying spinnakers. Automatically he thought they must be contestants in the Observer race, and it was only later that he realised they were travelling west and must have been in the race from Bermuda to Spain which followed the Newport-Bermuda race – won for Britain by Ron Amey's *Noryema* during June.

After *Flying Angel*'s arrival there followed a succession of French boats, which began to seem inevitable. Yves Olivaux was led home by Joel Charpentier in *Wild Rocket*, and followed in by the Swiss-with-strong-French-overtones Guy Piazzini, with Pierre Chassin's *Concorde* coming in a day later. Charpentier made light his passage in the big schooner, except to complain of lack of wind.

Piazzini, too, reported an uneventful trip. His main problem had been the beard he grew on the way over. He found it irritated terribly. Chassin sailed up to the end of the jetty as if he were bringing a dinghy in, his Alsatian dog Billy barking joyfully at the thought of being able to get ashore again.

Just as *Concorde* came in under sail, Bruce Webb's *Gazelle* was also being edged up to the quay under tow. It was Sunday 23 July, which happened to be Webb's 51st birthday, so the greetings by his wife and daughter were particularly enthusiastic. Or they would have been, if he had not also decided to join the beard-growers during the passage. His wife Joan was appalled. 'Doesn't he look awful,' she cried. The other thing that Mrs Webb noticed immediately was that Bruce had lost the paunch that he was sporting before the start of the race.

It turned out that the flattened stomach was not just the result of the hard work of keeping the boat going across the Atlantic: Webb's eating habits had changed. Before the race started he had been over-eating because of nervousness. Once he was sailing the overstimulated appetite righted itself. Certainly he looked extremely fit at the end of the voyage.

So, too, did John Holtom, the Warwickshire farmer who had shown a quiet determination to sail this race whatever the cost. He finished an hour behind Bruce Webb, to take 21st place in just over 36 days – a creditable performance for a cruising 34-footer.

On handicap, these placings couldn't compare with the next yacht home – Guy Hornett's little 26 foot Kingfisher, *Blue Smoke*. She arrived on the morning of Monday 24 July, having crossed the ocean in the remarkable time of under 37 days. Because she was very much an estuary cruising type of boat, with bilge keels, the handicapping committee had been very generous to *Blue Smoke*. They calculated that she would need 29½ days more than the scratch boat to get to Newport. The result was that Guy Hornett shot to the head of the monohull handicap list, displacing McMullen's *Binkie II*. And he was never beaten.

Hornett himself made very little fuss about the voyage. I found him that Monday morning, calmly pouring milk on his breakfast cereal as though he finished a transatlantic race every weekend. There was little to say about the trip, he said. The boat went very well and he was quite lucky with weather. When I saw the co-ordinates of *Blue Smoke*'s passage I began to see what he meant. Hornett had sailed the little 26-footer along the great circle route, keeping her up around the 45th parallel for most of the second half of the passage and only turning south for Newport when to keep on would have taken him straight into the Nova Scotian coastline.

In the comparatively mild conditions of the 1972 race, this policy had paid off well. But that is not to gainsay the courage and determination which lay behind the decision to take the little boat along a northern route. And this from a man who gave up his first attempt at a qualifying cruise in *Blue Smoke* because the conditions were too rough and the skipper was prepared to admit that he was very frightened. I left Newport that day on my way back to London, and one of my clearest memories on the return journey was of the submariner sailor who so modestly made the handicap for monohulls his own by an admirable feat of sailing.

There was a pause of more than a day before another competitor crossed the line at Brenton Reef. And it was a pause in which many people were summing up possibilities and beginning to ask questions. What could have become of Phil Weld, the likeable American with the big trimaran? The other multihulled yachts had all done so well, surely a 44 foot trimaran should be in before a 26 foot cruising boat? And where were the other two girls? The news of both *Komodor* and *P.S.* had been very thin throughout the five weeks the race had now run. But there was no point in jumping to unwarranted conclusions. Hadn't Tom Follett and Sir Francis Chichester already shown us the dangers of that? And hadn't Michael Richey proved in 1968 that the North Atlantic could contain some very big holes in its winds?

Sure enough, a couple of days later *Trumpeter* arrived at Newport with Phil Weld still full of his usual thigh-slapping bonhomie. He had found more than his fair share of calms, and the last week of his 39½ day passage had been made all the more difficult by a broken centreboard. He did report one incident which seemed comic in retrospect but must have been deadly serious at the time. When *Trumpeter* was near the Azores, her skipper had climbed the mast in a chair to mend a shredded mast shroud. But the down haul for the chair cleated itself below and Weld found himself stuck half way. Eventually he had to clamber out of the chair and slither down the mast to safety. He made light of it at Newport, but it seemed significant that he had needed two days of quiet going after that to recover.

Trumpeter arrived on the Wednesday of the week that began with *Blue Smoke*'s unexpected appearance. The day before had seen two Englishmen and a West German cross the line. First of the three was Wolf Kirchner, the German who had started the morning after everyone else. He had made good time in his little 32 foot sloop, but not quite such impressive progress as Richard Clifford in *Shamaal*, who was 25th to finish, three hours later.

Clifford's Contessa 26 had crossed in 38½ days, following a classic rhumb line course, unlike *White Dolphin* which had gone right down to 35 degrees north after passing through the Azores. The Marine lieutenant's only perilous moment had been when a freak wave hit *Shamaal* just as he was baling out the cockpit. Clifford was very nearly swept overboard, but managed to grab a guardrail as he was lifted bodily out of the boat.

Between *White Dolphin* and *Shamaal* came *Ron Glas*, with Jock McLeod delighted to report that he had fulfilled his ambition – he never used his oilskins and he needed to reef his big lugsails only three times on the whole trip. He too had gone well south, actually passing below the 34th parallel on one day. It certainly seemed to pay off as far as the weather was concerned.

Trumpeter was beaten home on the Wednesday by another American, Bob Lancy Burn in *Blue Gipsy*. This 28 foot sloop had also been given a generous allowance by the handicapping committee, so Burn's passage of 39 days 8½ hours put him into 2nd place and moved *Binkie II* one more position down the list for the monohull trophy. And that was the way they stayed.

Three more medium sized sloops finished that week: the second West German, Claus Hehner in *Mex*, Italy's Ambrogio Fogar in *Surprise*, and Pat Chilton in *Mary Kate of Arun*. Hehner had followed the northern route four years earlier, but this time he went the Azores way, passing north of the islands and then running along between the 36th and 39th parallels. It provided an interesting contrast to his 1968 course, and despite the extra mileage put him into Newport just under a day more quickly.

Fogar's crossing was fraught with problems, for he broke his rudder when close to the Azores and sailed the rest of the way without it. He reported in Newport that he had blown out four foresails and broken a gooseneck. By the time he arrived at the finishing line the only intact sails he had were a storm jib, a small genoa, and an undersized main.

As July turned into August the arrivals became sparser. I was able to write in *The Observer* for Sunday 6 August that just four boats had arrived in Newport during the previous seven days. First of these was the smallest boat to cross the line at that stage – Eric Sumner's Folkboat *Francette*. She made the crossing in just over 43 days, and Sumner said he had experienced a very mixed passage. He made good time to the Azores and then was stuck in a three-day calm, followed by a splendid week's run

of 1,000 miles. Then more calms off Nantucket cost him a couple of days. Still, he finished quickly enough to move into 8th place in the monohull handicap list.

Two days later the second Pole, Zbigniew Puchalski, arrived in his old and faithful *Miranda*, and then came the third and last West German, Heiko Krieger in *Tinie*. Another gap of two days, and then the last of the Americans, Jerry Cartwright, crossed the line in *Scuffler III*. Not surprisingly, Cartwright failed to beat the time of *Scuffler III*'s sister ship *Rob Roy*, which was sailed to Newport in 1968 by Stephen Pakenham in 42 days. But if one allows for the time that Cartwright lost while having his leak repaired in Falmouth, the two crossings would work out about even.

When *Lauric* crossed the line three days later, the elapsed time since the start had topped 50 days, and some concern was being expressed about the remaining yachts still at sea. However, Christopher Elliott gave little cause for worry because he had not left Plymouth until 4 July, so his actual time from Plymouth to Newport was a creditable 34½ days.

Next in was Andrew Spedding in the 28 foot sloop *Summersong*. He too had lost time through his collision soon after the start, so a week should really be taken off his elapsed time of just under 52 days. Third man in on 8 August was David Blagden with the smallest boat of all, *Willing Griffin*. When I spoke to Blagden on the transatlantic telephone he sounded full of vitality and very pleased with his 52½ day passage, apart from having lost about three days putting in to the Azores to change his polluted drinking water. His main concern had been bed-sores, for his boat was so small that he had to do everything sitting or lying down.

'Nothing broke, nothing jammed, nothing was carried away,' he told me proudly. 'We didn't even start a stitch in the sails. I had some phenomenal days, including one when I travelled 133 miles – not bad for a boat that's 17 feet 3 inches on the waterline.'

After *Griffin* sailed in there was a gap of five days and the worriers really got to work, especially about the two lady sailors still at sea – Teresa Remiszewska and Anne Michailof. But there was no cause for alarm: they arrived just over 24 hours apart on 13 and 14 August. The Polish singlehander was first to reach Newport, after 57 days at sea – a long passage for a 42 foot boat. She appeared to be very tired and *Komodor* looked as though it had endured a pretty rough passage, but the skipper was soon restored to health in the company of a distant cousin now living in America whom she had not seen for 15 years.

Anne Michailof's *P.S.* crossed the line after 58 days and six hours, just two hours ahead of Michael Richey's *Jester*. Richey had said in Plymouth that he intended to take a much more direct route this time than the experimental trade winds way he tried in 1968, but he was still nearly a day slower – an indication of the continuing feebleness of the winds in the North Atlantic.

When the 60 day time limit expired at noon BST, 16 August, only three sailors and their yachts had failed to complete the course: Martin Wills in *Casper*, Richard Konkolski in *Nike* and Peter Crowther in the 1908 gaff cutter *Golden Vanity*. Konkolski and Wills soon followed in, and as this book went to press, only Crowther's *Old Lady of the Sea* was still on the way.

So the last competitors were accounted for, and the fleet finally dispersed from Newport. Many boats were on their way home long before the tail-enders appeared, of course. But there was one feeling common to all as they sailed away from Narragansett Bay: the 1972 race had been the biggest and the best of the series. It had forged many new friendships, proved many new boats. And for some it poured new fuel on a flame that had burned brightly before. I met Bob Miller in Cowes at the beginning of August. 'I have been in touch with Captain Shaw at the Royal Western,' he said. 'I'm definitely going again next time.' Suddenly I remembered that three of the sailors I had seen triumphant in Newport – Marc Linski, Guy Piazzini, and Alain Gliksman – had all failed to finish the course in 1968, and I became even more aware of the compulsive character of the challenge to sail the North Atlantic singlehanded.

16 Trick's End

Life, said Samuel Butler, is the art of drawing sufficient conclusions from insufficient premises. Yet when it comes to drawing sufficient conclusions about the 1972 Observer race there seems to be almost a superfluity of premises. Every competitor has a different story of the ocean and its hazards; every boat has reacted differently to the challenge of the Atlantic.

But several sufficient – or perhaps we would say significant – conclusions emerge very clearly from the amorphous mass of evidence that builds up when 55 solo sailors attempt the North Atlantic crossing. And the most important is clearly that 1972 was the year of the multihull. Just seven multihulled yachts crossed the line at Plymouth on 17 June – five trimarans and two catamarans. The five trimarans all finished, the two catamarans came to grief – one, as we know, through no fault of the skipper's. The results? First, 3rd, 5th, 6th, and 27th. And if Bill Howell had finished in the 5th place which was rightfully his, a multihull would have taken 7th place too.

It was certainly a triumph that few could have anticipated in the light of the disastrous showing by the multihulled yachts in 1968. Then there were 13 cats and tris among the 35 starters, and only 5 of them survived. Why should there be such a complete turnabout in just four years? Well, the weather played a very big part in it, of course. If the 1972 fleet had experienced the same conditions as those 35 yachts which contested the 1968 race, things might well have been different. On the other hand, many a multihull enthusiast (and there were plenty to make the point in Newport) would say that the latest crop of multihulls were just as well-equipped to face the crossing, no matter what the conditions, as their monohull rivals – the new version of the 500-mile qualifying cruise had enforced that.

Certainly, many lessons had been learned from the failure of earlier trimarans and catamarans – one had only to look at the very rugged construction of *Pen Duick IV* and *Cap 33* to see that. As Martin Minter-Kemp said to me, 'I was sure the victory was bound to come. It was only a question of development. The multis this time deserved to do well because they were well put together. What gets through the net now is pretty good. At one time the lunatic fringe thought a multihull could be built for peanuts. They built boats that went fast and fell to pieces when it blew force 6. But now we know that multis cannot be built for peanuts, and when they are properly built they are very potent machines.'

And not necessarily potent machines in the sense of yachts built specially for ocean racing. Probably the most significant arrival in the first ten boats home was Gerard Pestey's trimaran *Architeuthis*. Very much a cruising yacht, this huge and somewhat cumbersome-looking multihull sailed to Newport in $27\frac{1}{2}$ days, and finished less than an hour behind the specially-designed *Three Cheers*. Undoubtedly Pestey had had his share of good fortune, but he also had a good, strong boat, which he made competitive by denuding it of every piece of unnecessary equipment (he actually lightened her by four tons!) and then sailed extremely competitively. I know of no other boat in the fleet which bettered Pestey's best day's sailing of 269 miles.

The other aspect of multihulls which was fully tested by the 1972 race was their safety in collision situations. We have already studied Bill Howell's last-lap disaster in some detail. It is enough here simply to add Howell's own final comment – as forthright and pithy as ever. 'I know this much: if I had been in this collision in a monohull, I would have sunk like a stone.'

The popularity of the multihull among sailing enthusiasts – in England anyway – has been very like the popularity of the political parties between general elections. After *Toria* won the Round Britain race in 1966 there was a definite 'swing' towards the multis. When so many came to grief in the 1968 Observer Singlehanded, the opposite reaction set in. And when a big monohull won the 1970 Round Britain – the *Ocean 71* crewed by Robin Knox-Johnston and Leslie Williams – then it seemed that the death knell of the multihull was sounding. Certainly the numbers of multihull craft exhibited at the International Boat Show in London in January 1972 showed a sharp decline.

Now we can expect the new swing of the pendulum. The multis have proved themselves all over again. Maybe Martin Minter-Kemp will even find a sponsor to back his plan for an 83 foot tri! The next pointer to the acceptability of multihull craft will be the number entered for the 1974 Round Britain. It should be a very interesting fleet. I understand that both *Trumpeter* and *Cap 33* will cross the Atlantic once more to join it.

The other really significant point about the 1972 race is the triumph of the French. To take the first three places, mop up the multihull handicap trophy, provide the first woman home, and annex the under-35 feet award as well is little short of a whitewash. One can only marvel at the determination and skill of this talented group of solo sailors.

Is there any particular reason for their overwhelming success in this race? Perhaps one key personality lies at the centre of it all – Eric Tabarly. He was the first man to build a boat specially for an Observer race – *Pen Duick II* for the triumph of 1964. He was the man who set the high standards of dedication and will to win which all the others try to match. He developed the boat and trained the skipper that won the race this time.

Talking with the French contestants, one often finds the name Tabarly cropping up in the conversation. Whether they know him or have sailed with him or not, each one of his compatriots is aware of the way he set out to win in 1964, and how he has won so much more since. Each one reflects some of his utter determination. Think of Linski and Olivaux pushing on when handicapped and in pain; think of Colas going over the side to repair his self-steering in a gale; think of Marie-Claude Fauroux pressing on relentlessly in *Aloa VII*, and think of Alain Gliksman getting the tiny *Toucan* across the ocean fast enough to finish eighth in front of boats half as big again. Each of them showed something of the Tabarly spirit, the vital urge not just to cross the ocean, but to race every inch of the way.

It is a mentality which seems exclusive to the French at this stage. Perhaps others will develop it. I am not saying, of course, that people like Brian Cooke, Tom Follett, and Martin Minter-Kemp were not trying hard. Of course they were. But, nice people that they are, they possibly lacked that edge of ruthlessness which marked the French. Some would say they are better for it, because it is, after all, a sporting event with no actual financial reward at the end. Not everyone would want to fashion themselves to the Tabarly model. Still, the fact remains that the ruthless approach has brought the results. Those who want to contest the main prizes next time must be aware of what they are up against.

Of course, some of the Frenchmen had the biggest boats as well. Of the eleven yachts measuring more than 50 feet in the starting fleet, the French had the biggest representation with five: *Pen Duick IV*, *Vendredi 13*, *Cap 33*, *Architeuthis*, and *Wild Rocket*. They finished 1st, 2nd, 3rd, 6th, and 16th. Britain had three, of which two survived: *British Steel* and *Strongbow*, finishing 4th and 7th. The others were Dijkstra's unlucky *Second Life*, Faggioni's *Sagittario*, and Ferris's *Whisper*. Obviously extra length paid off. Indeed, it made some of the other competitors think that perhaps it was time some sort of limit or handicap might be put on the biggest boats. Was *Vendredi 13* really out of keeping in a race of this kind? I think not. The fact is that for all her huge length she did not win the race. This must be encouragement to any singlehander with aspirations to the major trophy in years to come. Perhaps we are now near the limit of what one man can handle effectively.

One skipper I spoke to in Newport thought there would be a very good case to be made for imposing a penalty on any hull length over, say, 50 feet. It would certainly encourage the sort of people who have fairly conventional-size boats to think that, for example, each foot over the prescribed 50 would carry a penalty of one hour. In that case a 128 foot schooner like Terlain's would have to get in three days and six hours ahead of any other boat to be sure of winning. But there's the rub: the world would no longer know if the first boat home was indeed the winner. We would be back to the tangled and unsatisfactory system of IOR racing, where one has to wait for all the boats to get home and then the deliberations of the people working out the time correction factors before a definite result can be established.

My own vote is for keeping the race exactly as it is. Let the monsters come, and let the smaller craft prove that they are capable of making up the difference in waterline length by better design, better equipment, or simply better seamanship. The object of the race is to encourage the development of suitable boats and gear, supplies and technique for singlehanded ocean crossings under sail. By making the smaller boats face the challenge of the monsters on level terms, that development continues to be encouraged. By giving an arbitrary assistance to boats of a certain length, that development could well be stultified.

Of course, highly developed boats – especially highly developed big boats – cost a lot of money. And for most people that means the need to find a sponsor. There are still sponsors to be found, even if the rules for the 1972 race made the search even more difficult than before. I trust that is a situation which will improve for the 1976 race. Fairly obviously, the slightly vague wording of the 1972 rule about sponsorship was open to a number of different interpretations. In practice a firm producing a cider called 'Strongbow' were able to call their boat by that name, whereas a firm making cigarettes called 'Pieter Stuyvesant' were not allowed to call their boat by that name, even though each was a historical character (and the latter actually had much more significance in a race to America since he was the man who founded New York). This seems unfair.

What would happen, supposing the rule remained as it was this time, if a yacht were entered by China and called, say, *Hong Fu*? Are the organisers going to despatch a man to Peking to check whether 'Hong Fu' is a well-known brand of bird's nest soup? No, the sensible solution, it would seem, is to allow the yachts to be called whatever the skipper or backer likes, as long as the painted name is decently proportional to the size of the hull. We did have *British Steel* in the 1972 race. It did not really seem any more commercialised an entry than any of the others. I feel sure the same would apply if the fleet were scattered with boats called *Stork*, *Gumption*, or even *Littlewood's Pools*!

A final point on the rules. The fierce one that boats arriving late in Plymouth must start when all the others had gone was sensibly modified at the last moment by the Race Committee. Let's hope it stays modified for the 1976 race. Of course, you must have a measure of discipline about collecting in Plymouth, otherwise boats would be arriving at any old time, and the inspection and handicapping committees would have an impossible task. But a time penalty should be enough.

The mention of handicapping brings us to another topic that was debated loud and long in Newport.

The complaint, mainly from the French faction, was that some of the handicaps set were totally unrealistic. As we have seen, certain figures were amended at the last moment, but even so those that remained seemed unaccountably kind to some and depressing to others. Now that the race is over there is little point in scratching over the old ground in detail, but I would suggest that Gliksman's feat in getting *Toucan* to Newport in 28½ days deserved better recognition than to be lost half way down the handicap list. In fact, to have won the handicap for monohulls Gliksman would have needed to take another 8½ days off his time – in other words, to have beaten *Pen Duick IV* to Newport. This is plainly ridiculous.

Nevertheless, I draw the line at support for the motion raised by some French sailors in Newport that the Royal Western Yacht Club should have a party to present the handicap award before the race starts from Plymouth!

Though my chapter on 'Alarums and excursions' is one of the longest in this book, the 1972 race was actually a big improvement on the 1968 event on the score of casualties. Then, 35 yachts started the race and 16 – nearly half – failed to finish the course. Of the 1972 starting fleet of 55, all but 12 arrived in Newport. One of those was an unavoidable collision, and two were brought about by the illness of the crews, so effectively only nine boats were found wanting. But of those seven suffered dismasting. It seems a high proportion, considering that for the most part the weather for this race was not unkind. The mast is obviously a component that every singlehander must be able to rely on, especially if he is going to be driving his boat to windward. No doubt the entrants for the next race will have read and marked the number of broken sticks this time.

Naturally, the new ruling requiring a 500 mile cruise has made a difference in the quality of the boats entered in 1972 compared with those four years earlier. That is certainly one of the Royal Western's decisions that everyone will applaud. There is no doubt that boats for this race were much better prepared than ever before, and that high success rate proves it.

What else was new this time? The Russian trawler fleet certainly played a much more dramatic part in the final stages than had ever been the case previously. Coinciding with a particularly foggy July in

Rhode Island Sound, this tightly packed fleet proved a very real hazard when the yachts were already hampered by light winds and tidal currents. I lost count of the number of singlehanders who told me that the worst part of the whole trip had been the last two or three days getting into Newport.

And the Russian fleet ties up with another innovation in the 1972 race – a handicap trophy for the multihulls. Bill Howell would certainly have won that trophy if he had finished the course in *Tahiti Bill*. But maybe it will be more meaningful in 1976, when there should be many more multihull yachts entered, and maybe Bill Howell will at last win a trophy all his own.

Another major difference in the next race in the series could be the number of American boats entered. It has always seemed strange that the target country should be so poorly represented, but the climate is certainly changing in the United States. Newspaper, radio, and television coverage of the 1972 race was much wider than ever before over there, and considerable interest among the yachting fraternity was stirred up by the constant coverage of the event given by the mushrooming magazine *Sail* and the enthusiasm of its editor Murray Davis, who actually lives in Newport.

If the plans which I began to work out during my stay in Newport develop, 1976 could well see the state of Rhode Island sponsoring a race for American entries from Newport to Plymouth starting about five weeks before the Observer race. It would be for fully crewed boats and would start on 4 May 1976, exactly 200 years since Rhode Island declared its independence from British rule (the colony went independent two months ahead of the other 12 in the original union). That would certainly encourage more Americans to enter.

It would be pleasant, too, to see more entries from Eastern European nations. The four representatives of Poland and Czechoslovakia charmed all their new friends on both sides of the Atlantic. Perhaps they will be reinforced next time round. The race is certainly a truly international event now. It is even fully reported in Warsaw, as Chris Baranowski proved to me when his batch of press clippings arrived.

But before we get too involved in plans for 1976, what else is there to learn from the 1972 race? Dr Glin Bennett will certainly learn a great deal from the many questionnaire cards he collected from competitors in Newport, but it will take a long time to sift the evidence carefully and come to scientifically justified conclusions. In the meantime, Glin was delighted to find that most of the people asked had diligently filled in their cards every day. And he was not at all put out by those who said they became so fed up with the whole idea that they threw the whole lot over the side.

There's an interesting lesson to be learned, too, from the different routes that the singlehanders followed. A far greater proportion of the fleet followed the Azores route this time – no doubt encouraged by Tom Follett's good showing in the 1968 race after taking that track. And once again the Azores route provided the third place man. But I think the skippers really determined to put up the fastest times will still opt for the most direct route, unless, of course, their boat is a multihull. Despite Follett's unfortunate experience this time, the good speeds of *Cap 33*, *Tahiti Bill*, and *Architeuthis* along the southern course support the theory that a multihull has a better chance of good reaching winds down there as long as it can keep south of the contrary Gulf Stream.

What, then, are the final lessons to be learned from 1972? That a multihull can win; that adequate preparation is just as important as determination and skill in the skipper; that widely differing routes can result in very similar times; and, above all, that the Atlantic will always be an enigma as far as weather is concerned.

You do not beat the Atlantic. You cross by its courtesy. To some it will reach out a gentle and helpful hand. To others, like Minter-Kemp and Bob Miller, it will show a sudden fit of temper. To still others, like Follett and Phil Weld, it will be capricious and fickle. The singlehander must accept its many moods and make of them what he can. Alain Colas certainly made the best of every opportunity he had during his record passage of under 21 days. It seems impossible to believe that anyone will ever take such a huge slice out of the record time again.

But then, remember Jean-Yves Terlain saying that he thinks he can improve the performance of *Vendredi 13* by at least 20 per cent. Think of Martin Minter-Kemp saying he thought *Strongbow* could be refined to the point where she could win next time. See all the lessons that yacht designers must have learned from this race and consider how they might be implemented in a race-winning yacht for next time. Why, even before half the fleet was home Dick Newick was talking in Newport about the possibility of a boat with five hulls being a feasible proposition for the next race. With hydrofoils, of course. Now if it worked, such a boat really could get the record down to . . . let's see, it has gone 40 days, 27, 25, 20½ . . . gosh, we might one day see a solo sailor getting to America in less than a fortnight!

And there lies the fascination of this great and growing race. There is absolutely no limit to its potential, both in the boats that enter and in the people that sail them. I was privileged to move among and know a group of outstanding individuals during the summer of 1972. Without exception, they showed a generosity and humour above the usual level. I suspect these qualities rise to the surface as a man gains that deep inner knowledge of himself that comes only when he is cut off from all other influences and assistance. I know that I shall always remember those happy and self-contained people and see in them the reflections of Slocum and Dumas, Moitessier and Rose; indeed of all the many brave seamen who became bigger and better people because they had sailed solo to America.

Final Placings in 1972 Observer Singlehanded

Place	Yacht	Crew	Country	Elapsed time D	H	M
1	Pen Duick IV	Alain Colas	France	20	13	15
2	Vendredi 13	Jean-Yves Terlain	France	21	05	14
3	Cap 33	Jean-Marie Vidal	France	24	05	40
4	British Steel	Brian Cooke	Britain	24	19	28
5	Three Cheers	Tom Follett	US	27	11	04
6	Architeuthis*	Gerard Pestey	France	28	11	55
7	Strongbow	Martin Minter-Kemp	Britain	28	12	46
8	Toucan	Alain Gliksman	France	28	12	54
9	Sagittario*	Franco Faggioni	Italy	28	23	05
10	Whisper	Jim Ferris	US	29	11	15
11	Isles du Frioul*	Marc Linski	France	30	02	45
12	Polonez	Chris Baranowski	Poland	30	16	55
13	Binkie II	Mike McMullen	Britain	31	18	10
14	Aloa VII*	Marie-Claude Fauroux	France	32	22	51
15	Flying Angel	Jock Brazier	Britain	33	09	21
16	Wild Rocket	Joel Charpentier	France	34	13	38
17	Aloa I	Yves Olivaux	France	34	17	30
18	Cambronne	Guy Piazzini	Switzerland	35	10	24
19	Concorde	Pierre Chassin	France	36	01	19
20	Gazelle	Bruce Webb	Britain	36	02	07
21	La Bamba of Mersea	John Holtom	Britain	36	04	30
22	Blue Smoke	Guy Hornett	Britain	36	21	26
23	White Dolphin	Wolf Kirchner	W Germany	38	07	17
24	Ron Glas	Jock McLeod	Britain	38	09	50
25	Shamaal	Richard Clifford	Britain	38	10	30
26	Blue Gipsy	Bob Lancy Burn	US	39	08	30

Place	Yacht	Crew	Country	Elapsed time D H M
27	Trumpeter	Phil Weld	US	39 13 25
28	Mex*	Claus Hehner	W Germany	40 08 23
29	Surprise	Ambrogio Fogar	Italy	41 04 45
30	Mary Kate of Arun	Pat Chilton	Britain	41 17 17
31	Francette	Eric Sumner	Britain	43 09 38
32	Miranda	Zbigniew Puchalski	Poland	45 10 05
33	Tinie	Heiko Krieger	W Germany	46 15 30
34	Scuffler III	Jerry Cartwright	US	49 02 00
35	Lauric	Christopher Elliott	Britain	51 14 33
36	Summersong	Andrew Spedding	Britain	51 23 05
37	Willing Griffin	David Blagden	Britain	52 11 06
38	Komodor	Teresa Remiszewska	Poland	57 03 18
39	Jester	Michael Richey	Britain	58 08 18
40	P.S.*	Anne Michailof	France	59 06 12

* Yachts subject to penalties for late arrival, late completion of qualifying cruise, or crossing the line before the start gun. Times shown are corrected.

At noon 16 September, when the 60 day period of the race was completed, *Nike* (Richard Konkolski), *Casper* (Martin Wills), and *Golden Vanity* (Peter Crowther) had not yet reached Newport.

Monohull Handicap Trophy – Final Placings

Position	Yacht	Corrected time D H M	Position	Yacht	Corrected time D H M
1	Blue Smoke	7 07 06	15	British Steel	16 18 08
2	Blue Gipsy	9 08 30	16	Tinie	17 01 10
3	Binkie II	10 13 30	17	Polonez	17 09 35
4	La Bamba of Mersea	12 09 10	18	Gazelle	18 14 07
5	Shamaal	13 03 10	19	Mary Kate of Arun	18 17 17
6	Flying Angel	14 07 01	20	Sagittario	19 08 25
7	Aloa VII	14 18 11	21	Isles du Frioul	19 16 05
8	Francette	15 02 18	22	Cambronne	20 15 04
9	Whisper	15 06 35	23	Mex	21 01 03
10	Willing Griffin	15 15 46	24	Vendredi 13	21 05 14
11	Ron Glas	15 19 30	25	Scuffler III	21 21 20
12	Toucan	15 22 34	26	Surprise	22 12 05
13	Aloa I	16 12 15	27	Concorde	22 17 59
14	White Dolphin	16 14 37	28	Strongbow	22 21 04

Position	Yacht	Corrected time D H M	Position	Yacht	Corrected time D H M
29	Miranda	26 10 05	32	Summersong	28 11 05
30	Wild Rocket	27 06 18	33	P.S.	35 10 52
31	Jester	27 06 58	34	Komodor	39 01 58

Lauric was not given a handicap figure as she did not start until 4 July.

Multihull Handicap Trophy – Final Placings

Position	Yacht	Corrected time D H M	Position	Yacht	Corrected time D H M
1	Pen Duick IV	16 19 15	4	Architeuthis	19 21 35
2	Cap 33	17 10 20	5	Trumpeter	31 15 45
3	Three Cheers	19 17 04			